Love Me

Glenda Olsen

Copyright © 2024 by Glenda Olsen

All rights reserved.

No portion of this book may be reproduced in any form without written permission from the publisher or author, except as permitted by U.S. copyright law.

Contents

1. Chapter one — 1
2. Chapter two — 5
3. chapter three — 9
4. Chapter four — 13
5. chapter five — 17
6. Chapter Six — 22
7. Chapter seven — 27
8. chapter eight — 32
9. chapter nine — 37
10. chapter ten — 42
11. Chapter eleven — 48
12. Chapter twelve — 53
13. Chapter thirteen — 59
14. Chapter fourteenth — 64
15. Chapter fifteen — 68

16. Chapter sixteenth — 72
17. Chapter seventeenth — 78
18. chapter eighteenth — 83
19. Chapter nineteenth — 88
20. chapter twenty — 93
21. Chapter twenty one — 98
22. chapter twenty two — 102
23. Chapter tweenty-three — 107
24. Chapter twenty-four — 112
25. Chapter twenty-five — 117
26. chapter twenty six — 122
27. Chapter twenty seven — 127
28. chapter twenty eight — 133
29. Chapter tweenty-nine — 139
30. Chapter thirty — 145

Chapter One

Chapter one

Arabella POV

"Mom are you serious?!" I asked my mom in a very enthusiastic tone.

"Yup sweety! So you be good in your senior year and I can promise you, We will send you to the school of your choice!" She said while she hug me.

I have a very loving and supportive parents. I used to get what I want but in return of doing something good and they will reward me. I am A+ student and proud to be a nerd. Those classic big rim round eye glass? Wearing only simple sweater and jeans, no make up just natural, yes that's me people!.

Mom used to convince me to show the world my beauty. Don't blame me it's my mom word ok? I don't even know why she said beauty. I don't have any of it. I swear I feel pity of my parents since they both have beautiful genes but their one and only daughter turns out to be ugly duckling!

"Thanks mom! I love you so much and dad too!" I chuckle while I pull off from her hug.

"Sweetie, you are the best daughter we could ever asked. Your brothers are damn lucky to have you as their big sister" mom said.

"Thanks man! I go to school mom. I might get late if I don't start heading there!" I said as I slung my backpack on my right shoulder. Then I kissed her and went off to school.

I so excited and nervous at the same as I step inside the campus. Not because I am new here but every one eyes turns to me and I wonder why?. I just let it go and went straight ahead to my first class.

I reached my room and plop in the first row. Not minding the creepy stares that my classmates gives me. Not new to me since I been used to that kind of stares since my first school. Thank God the teacher arrived just exact time the bell rang.

"Good morning class. I am your teacher. I am Teacher Gisele your science teacher. I'm looking forward for cooperation since our subject compose of group activities. And that's what I intend to do until the semester end. Am I clear?", Then she began to explain about this and that.

When we are in middle of class discussion the door burst open and reveal the most handsome guy I ever seen in my entire life. He walked in front me like he is god. He's freaking sexy and handsome although I am used to see handsome guys since my brothers are all handsome, not to brag ok?.

I secretly glance on his direction and I saw him sit beside the girl with blonde hair and she put her hands on his thigh and chest. What a flirt! I snorted and shake my head while I divert my attention to the teacher whose practically nagging him but it's seem he doesn't heard anything at all.

"Mr. Ashton Carter, please behave and Ms. Elle Davis keep in your hands on yourself, don't wander else someone body" then teacher while she eyed both of them. Thank God this teacher has some senses.

Ashton just shrugged his shoulder and the girl Elle name thank God she keep her little respect to herself. Just like that the class resume and without notice the bell rang. The students busy picking up their stuff and hurriedly went out. Time for my next class..

After I went to my second class the bell rang it's indicating that's it's lunch time.

I went to cafeteria and boy it's super huge and the food looks yummy. I take a line to pick out some food for me to eat. I look around for an empty seat and just my luck I saw at the corner with vacant one. I plop on it and began eating my precious food.

Someone took a sit the chair opposite of me and I saw a girl with a long black hair smiling towards me.

"Can I sit in here?" She asked me shyly.

"Sure!" Then I smiled in return to her.

"Are you new here? It seems like it's my first time I saw you!" She asked me while she take a bite of her burger.

"Yup! Just transfer here this year!" While I nodded my head.

"Do you want to be friends? I'm jasmine and you?" Then she offer her hand and I shake it.

"Nice to meet jasmine! I'm Arabella. Let's be friends then!" I smiled to her.

Then she suddenly stood up on her seat and plop beside me.

"Since where friends and you are new here! I will tell you about this school!" She said. Then her eyes wander around the cafeteria. "Did you see the guy whose sexy with blue eyes and blond hair? That's Ashton, he's the hottest guy on campus, guys and girls wanted to be with him. Like when your close to him it's like your popular. Then that girl sitter on her lap? That's Aliyah, she's a cheerleader and one of sluts here on campus. Those girls and boys together in their table stay away from them they're no good for us need" then she giggled to me.

"Yeah I keep that in mind!" I keep munching my food. "Want some fries?" I offer her. Then she immediately grab it and put in her mouth.

"Food is life for me! Hahahahah I can't say no to it!" Then we laughed together.

The bell and we clean our trash. We sprint to our next subject. Thank God we have the same last subject and that's history.

I text my mom and I am almost finish and it's my last subject for today. I didn't bother to look my way and I bump into someone. Because it's too sudden my books drops and even my eyes glass drop too. Shit!!!

"Sorry" I said while I bend down to pick up my things . I noticed the person I bump still standing infront of me. After collecting my things I straighten my clothes and look up, my breath almost hitch since I saw pair of beautiful blue eyes looking at me intensely. I cleared my throat to gain his attention.

"Sorry for bumping you. I didn't meant to!" I said while I bow my head to show how sorry I am.

He bend down to whisper something on my ears.

"Nerd take off that glasses it doesn't suit you at all" then he walk away from me.

I look at him shock and stunned. What the hell just happened???

Chapter Two

Chapter two

Ashton POV

I look up sky the since I am lying on the ground with a green grass on it. This is my natural hobby, skipping my class and just lay down here and not bother nor caring anything in this world.

I look at the side ways corner. I see girls giggling while gawking at me with their lustful smiles. Hmm... It's also natural sight to me . Every day I always have sensual offers from them not that I complaining though. It's just that , sometimes woman should have self respect and dignity to thierselves.

Yes! I am a man whore and play boy but I still want woman who will value her body more. I know... I know... It's contradict to what you expect of me right? What can I do? When they offer their selves to me I just grab the opportunity, it's not like I force them, they give it to me willingly.

I heard one of my talking on my side while they sitting on the grass. I am just contented listening to their non stop arguments.

"Oh come on! How about we make a bet! Huh?!" Xander said.

"What kind of bet is that?" Lucas said while his eyes dance with amusement on it.

"You know! Whoever knock the girl first win! What can you say?" Xander said while he laugh to what he said.

"Come on! Xander! What's the challenge on that? We all practically knock out almost of the girls in our campus? And you want to bet on it? Are you stupid?!!" Ethan said angrily. Now that's true!

The four of us are the most popular and influential guys in campus not just by our looks but also the vibes that's our parents has to the school too.

Since diaper days, the four of us has been friends because our family had been long time partner in business. So it's we been thick and thin although out the years.

"Hahaha... You think I didn't know about that moron? Of course I know" Xander said while he kick Ethan feet playfully

"Don't touch me you prick!" Ethan hiss at him. While swatting Xander feet.

"Shut up both of you!" I said

They all look at me and I raised my brow in confusion.

"What?" I said to them

"Now that I remember you talked to this girl yesterday? I mean that transfers student in our school!" Xander said while he caress his jaw

"So!" Lucas said non challant

"Ashton.. since your the first guy talked to her how about you make her fall for you and knock her up in my birthday party this year and that would be in December" Xander said while he's eyes glitter more because of amusement

"Then what do I get from this?" I asked them

"You can get anything you want from me" Xander said with confidence.

Oh! That's what I like...a bet and I think it would be fun.

"Ok I am taking your favorite red Audi the one that your dad gift to you to your last year birthday!" I said to him while my eyes dance with amusement too.

"Sure... I bet you can make her fall for you. I heard she's a nerd, good luck with that bro!" Xander said while laughing

Ethan and Lucas just shrugged their shoulders looking to us.

"Whatever! I will win this bet for sure!" I said with confidence

And with that we sealed our agreement. I will surely knock this girl even though nerds are not my thing.

After discussing our agreement I went to my next subject and would be physical education. I like this subject this I can freely play around and I live to play games, exercising is my top priority at early age I am able to obtain six pack in my torso.

I walked to my locker and grab a pair of my P.E uniform. I change my clothes in the changing rooms which located near my locker and went immediately to the gym of our school.

Just when I arrive in the gym, as usual the girls eyes are all on me. Boys are eyeing me with jealously. I make my way through the class and my eyes immediately snap to the nerd I bump yesterday. She's wearing P.E uniform which unexpectedly looks sexy on her.

My eyes take a peck on her abs and her long while legs is so damn sexy. Why did I not notice this? This girl is freaking sexy just minus her big round eye glasses. Maybe without it , she will be one of the most beautiful and popular girl in here. I look again to her and I saw her looking seriously to the teacher. She keep nodding her head and still oblivious to my eyes. Slowly she glance on my side and I smile to her.

"Hi!!!" I said while I scooter closer to her.

"Hello" she said then turning her attention again to the teacher.

"Class we will be playing volleyball, so we need to form 4 groups since you are all consist of 20 people in the class. Each team will have 5 members. So let's start regrouping you all." The teacher said enthusiastic

After done grouping we played volleyball. The teacher said to practise for ten minutes and after that we will play volleyball game. The game start after ten minutes, we win the first game. The second is which the nerd is on it. I noticed her team mates didn't let her participate in the practise. Maybe they wanted to bully this girl. Her team consist of Elli, Lucia, Gerald, Matt and her. Those two girls are pure evil.

The game started and the nerd position herself in front. Wow! When everyone are all excited to bully and humiliate her but it all turn to gone. Why? Because she hit the ball correctly. She's like a real or pro volleyball player. Our teacher is so amaze looking at her.

After the game, everyone look at her amazing and shock. She just walked naturally and grab her bottle bottle then drink. She wipe her dripping sweat in her neck slowly then she take off her eyeglasses everyone snap on her direction.

She has a pair of green eyes like emerald. She untied her ponytail and fix her hair. Her long shiny black hair cascading on her back. After she wipe her face she put back her eyes glass.

Man that was epic! She's one hell gorgeous. She just don't know or just blind to see how beautiful she is.

Chapter Three

chapter three

Arabella POV

After my physical education subject my body feel exhausted. Thank God my mother and father taught us to be physical active I was able to play volleyball well. I am not that pro it's just that it's my nature to love sport.

Indeed, so much for the love of sport our team won over all in our class. I can't wait to tell my parents about this. I bet they will jump of joy. Don't get me wrong my mom and dad are so supportive to me. Even my brothers too, although both of them are annoying and infuriating sometimes but I love all of them.

I went outside the gym and my breath almost hitch when a pair of blue eyes, stared at me. I noticed he's with his friends. They all glance at my direction and smile to me. Wow! What just happen? The four popular boys in school just smiled at me. Just wow!

I took a big stride wanting to be away from the place immediately because I can sense that girls jealous eyes are all on me. Why not? Those four just smile to a nerd like me.

I shake my head and head to the parking area where I park my red Ferrari car.

Yes I'm a nerd but that doesn't mean I don't have taste. Actually it's my parents gift to me in my 17th bday last year. But I only used it, to go to school since I am not into parties or going to shopping or even going to friends house, I'm just contented sitting in our library and read any sort of books that pin my interest.

"Hey!" My eyes quickly snap to the owner of the voice who happen to be on my side. My eyes went wide since it's Ashton walking beside me.

"Hi! Do you need something?" I asked him. While I try not to glance so much since it's too awkward.

"Hmm..I'm Ashton what's your name?" He asked me while he's eyes directed to me.

"I'm Arabella , you can call me Ara since my name is too long" I asked while I smile awkwardly to him.

"Sure Ara! Nice to meet you call me Ash, short for Ashton!" He said while we stop to shake hands. I quickly pull my hands since I can't stand the tingling sensation I feel.

"Can I get your number? If it's ok to you?" While his hands scratching at the back of his neck. I feel all my blood flows to my cheeks and I can feel how hot my cheeks right now. Who will not? It's freaking Ashton asking my damn number. Fuck!

"Sure!" He offer his phone and I take it. I type my number on it and name it as Ara. When I hand his phone to him, our hands accidentally brush each other and I know my cheeks as red as tomato right now.

"Thanks!... See you" he said smiling! His white teeth shows when he smile. He can be a model of toothpaste if he wants but I bet he will according to my friend he's son of billionaire just like my father.

"Yeah!" Then I walk again heading to my car. While he walk the other way and I can see his friends waiting for him at the bench sitting looking at us.

But before I could reach my car. My eyes widen when I saw a man approaching to me. What is he doing in here?

"Dad!!! What are you doing here?" My dad just casually walking in pathway of the parking area of our school. Girls gawking at him as if he's teenager. I don't blame them my dad is so handsome and still sexy.

"Princess! Is that how you greet your dad?" My dad scowl at me like he is hurt.

"Dad.....!" I whine to him while he is now infront of me. He open his arm and I jump to him. My dad really treat me like I'm still a baby.

"Princess.. I just want to see your new school, that's why me and you mom went here!" My dad said while the car open revealing my mom approaching us.

Boys are gawking at my mom. She's still beautiful and sexy as always no wonder dad is so madly in love to her. My dad never allow my mom go outside the house without him, talking about possessive here!.hahahahah. I see how my dad throw daggers to those boys eyeing my mom from head to foot. Shaking my head I just laugh. So much for having beautiful and handsome parents.

"Sweety! How's your 1st day? Do you like your new school?" While she kissed and hug me

"Mom why are you both here? Why does it feel like I am still kindergarten here? You don't need to see here, seriously?" I said dramatically

"Princess! We just want to see what kind of environment you have here. Anyway your brothers are here too!" My dad said. And eyes automatically went wide

"What? They're here too!oh my God!" Just like cue my brother's went out from the car and walked towards us. Girls are eyeing them like eating them literally since my brothers are both handsome. "Seriously guys!! Is this really necessary?" I asked them. Unbelievable Thai family of mine.

"Princess" Daniel and Emman said together. Then they hug me tightly

"Why are you here?" I asked them

"Of course your our princess. Is someone bully you here? You need to tell us ok? Even where far from you. Just one call or text will be there!" Daniel said.

"Seriously? As far as I remembered I am your older sister here! I should be the one protecting you not the other way around!" I remind them.

"Princess we boys protect you both of your mother. It's our duty being the boys of the family. It doesn't matter the age it's about obligation!" My dad interfere us

"Dad! Not you too!" I whine

"Come on stop it. You making my baby embarass let's continue this inside the car and we will go eat outside. Ok guys?" Thank God my mom stop our bickering.

We head to our car and my dad said our driver will pick up my car from school. So I went inside to our family car. But before I get inside I look around and I saw how people look at me and my family. So much for getting so much attention.

Chapter four

Ashton POV

I am shocked when I saw her family. So she's one of the elite too huh? I wonder why she's nerd.? He's father is no other than Archer Martin he's my dad rival in hotel business. He's a freaking billionaire at his young age and her mom own hospitals in the country and one of the best surgeon too. Just wow!

No wonder how all the students paying attentions to her family especially to her brothers. I didn't see them here , they must have attend different school from her. From the looks of it, she looks like a princess to her family. Why did she become nerd? Her mom, still look like in her early twenties, she's stunning and beautiful.

I shake my head and I turn my attention to my friends. We are all hanging in our usual bench together with sluts in school.

"Babe! How about we go somewhere?" She said while she sit on my lap.

"Elli stop it! I am not in the mood ok?" I said then I try to get her off to my lap.

"Come on babe I will make you better?" She said then biting her lower lips while her hands draws to my chest.

I shake my head and get up. I don't care if she stumble or not but I am not really in the mood and she can't understand a bit. I hate woman who are slut and only think about sex but no brains at all.

"What's with you? I am just want to make you feel better?" She whine to me and went to Xander.

"I gotta go guys! Mom texted me to come home early" then I get up and grab my bag pack. I grab my car key in my pocket and went to drive home. I just don't feel talking to them anymore.

I arrive in our house and I park my car in the garage. As always, our house is quite and empty, it always be only my mom and me at home, dad is always busy taking care of the business. I am not complaining but sometimes I wish he could spare some time for us.

Honestly the reason, I don't feel like talking to my friends awhile ago is that, when I saw that nerd family. I am envious of her that her parents have time to check on her on school. We have same billionaire father but her father manage to visit her and have time for his family while my dad keeps making himself billions. I don't understand why? I am only child, I can't spend it all. Why making so much money then?

That's the reason why I partied a lot and drinks alcohol but I don't do drugs ok? I am not that stupid!. Party, sex and alcohol that's the only thing I do. Mom always nagging me when she I smelled alcohol. She said I might die young from drinking too much at early age .

I understand her but what can I do? When I spend my time all alone in the house I feel like I'm going crazy.

I see my mom making something in the kitchen and I greeted her.

"Mom I'm home!" I said then I hug her

"Ash.. help mom cook for dinner ok? Dad said he will come home early" mom said happily.

"Wow! What's the occasion?" I said in a sarcastic tone.

"Ash he just want to eat together!" My mom explained

"Dad only went home early when there is occasion mom!" I said truthfully

"Yeah but people change Ash! Maybe he wants to come home early because he wants some time with us. Right?" Mom said in a bright smile.

I just shrugged my shoulder and went to my room to change into comfortable clothes. After that I help my mom cook dinner and set the dining table. As what my mom said dad really indeed come home early.

"Ash my boy" he said while he hug me then pat my back

"How are you dad?" I asked him

"Problem in business as always! But I can handle it. How about school?" He asked me while he loosen his tie.

"It's good!" I said shortly

"Ash this is your last year! I am hoping you will behave and less go to parties!" He said while he sit near my mom.

We begin to eat our dinner and I didn't bother to answer him. The only reason I partied it's because of him which he can never understand.

"Honey how about we go to vacation in Greece after Ash graduation? Like it means his graduation gift!" My mom happily said to my dad while she smile to him ear to ear.

"Of course I will book that in my calendar so I can vacant my time honey!" Dad said and kiss my mom cheeks.

"Dad are you still rival with Archer Martin?" I asked him suddenly

"We are not rival son, it's just that it's how the business world describes us. But Archer have different ways and different businesses. Though he also own a lot of hotels but he has restaurants, malls and hospitals. I on the other hand consentrate on hotel chain business and resorts!" My dad explained to me

"Are you friends?" I asked him which caught him off guard.

"Nope! We're just acquaintance but not close. We used to go same high school and college but never get close!" My dad said while thinking.

"Why?" I said

"Why sudden interest son? Did he do something to you?" He asked me while frowning

"Nope! It's just his daughter is my classmate!" I said truthfully

"Oh! His daughter might beautiful I guess? Since her mother and her father have a good genes right?" He said to me

" I don't know, we're not close and she's nerd" I told him

"Nerd? Really? Don't do something stupid son ok? Stay away from Archer daughter, I don't want any problem with him" my dad said

Too late dad because we already made a bet on her with my friends. I wanted to tell but of course I will not. I don't want to anger my dad.

chapter five

Arabella POV

After that incident in school I told my family not to go there especially when they are all together. It's so embarrassing, the fact that all my school mates seen them fetching me it's absolutely embarrassing. I could still feel my cheeks flush because of embarrassment. Good thing mom understand and she told me that, next time they will inform me.

It's been two weeks since the school opening. And I had only one become my friend and that is jasmine atleast I have one. Jasmine and I study together in the library and we eat together too in the cafeteria.

Right now I am sitting in the bench near the parking area. I texted Jasmine that I will wait for her here since she asked me if I can accompany her to go to bookstore because she have assignment in English. Then someone plop beside me and I thought it's jasmine but to my shock it's Ashton smiling towards me.

"Hey! Your alone?" He asked me

"Yeah! But my friend asked me to meet her here" I answered him

"Your going somewhere?" He asked me again

"Yeah! We're going to bookstore together cause we have assignment in English" I told him trying to calm my feelings. It's freaking Ashton talking to me. I know right now my cheeks are already red as shade of tomatoes since he keeps staring at me.

"I thought I could ask you to hang out with me. Like going to cafe?" He asked me while I look at him confused?

"Me?" I told him looking confused to him

"Of course! Your the only one here so it's you!" He said while he smile again. Oh man! That smile I think my panty gonna drop.

"Maybe next time!" I answer him. While I tackle the strand of my hair in my ears. I look at him shyly

I look at infront me cause I can't keep up staring each other. I notice Jasmine approaching towards me and I wave at her.

"My friend is here!" I told him

"Oh so next time? How about tomorrow? Same time here?" He ask me while he scratch the back of his neck.

"Yeah!" I smile to him sweetly

"I will go now! See you tomorrow!" Then he run while he's hands waving at me.

"What is that?" Jasmine ask. I didn't notice her beside me since I'm too focus on Ashton waving at me.

"That's Ashton!" I said while I smile to her.

"I know him ok? But why is he talking to you?" She asked persistently

"He asked me to go to cafe together tomorrow?" I told her shyly but I can't hide the smile on my face while sat cafe together, it feels so unreal.

"Stop blushing friend! Your so obvious I swear!" She said while she keep giggle

"Am I?" I ask her.

"Nah that's ok! Who never crush on Ashton? He's the most handsome and popular guy in school" she said while she guide me to my car. We are going to take my car because she said she never have ride Ferrari car on her entire life. Silly!!

****

I swear I never been so excited morning to come. I wake up earlier than my usual and put an effort for my clothes for the first time. I bet my mother will shock knowing I groom myself.

Then I went outside and I find my mom cooking something in the kitchen. When she look at me she is shock.

"Who are you? What happen to jeans and long oversize sweater?" My mom exclaimed

"Mom! I just change my clothes for today that's all!" I said

"Then take off that eyeglasses too!" She said then she take it off and put it farther from me. "Wear your contact lens" she continue when I try to snatch back my eyeglass

"But mom!!" I whine

"Hey what do my queen and princess do? " Dad said while kissing my mom. We did not noticed him.

"Look at your daughter! Isn't she beautiful hon?" Mom said to dad.

"Of course! She's our daughter after all!" Dad said proudly.

I roll my eyes to them and I sigh

"Mom give me my eyeglasses back. I don't like wearing lens. It's too itchy!" I said

"Come on! Just for today! Look how beautiful you are. Tell the truth you have date today right?" My mom said while she wiggle her brows to me. Dad immediately snap in my direction

"What date? I am not allowing you to do that!" My dad said loudly

"Dad it's just a friend asked me yesterday to go to cafe together!" I answered

"Is that a boy friend?" Daniel said I didn't notice him when he is in my back

"Tell me what's the name and I will beat the shit of him!" Emman said.

I scowl looking the three of them. This three will never change in being overprotective of me and mom.

"Guys it's not a date ok! He just ask me.... !!" Before I can finish my sentence the three of them look at me in a wide eyes.

"He???????" They three said in unison

"Hey! Stop that three of you!" My mom said while she playfully spank their heads.

"Mom she is asked by a guy?" Emman said

"Say no to him now!" Daniel voice boom

"No I don't have his number. And what is it to you guys. I am big enough ok? Can you just leave me alone!"I said to them.

"Princess tell us the name of the boy!" My dad said darkly

"Dad please have trust in me! Promise I will never hide anything to you all. Please? I love all of you and I will never betray your trust in me. I promise!" I told them sincerely

"Fine but only in cafe ok? After that go home! If your not home at 6pm. I will look for you and punch the guy princess. Remember that!" My dad said.

"Dad! Why are you allowing her to meet random guy;" Daniel said

"Yeah! She's too young what if!"Emman said

"Shut up both of you. Dad already permit so back off!" I said then I grab my bag and went outside the house. I forgot to take my eyeglasses from my mom. Anyway I need to be out of here since those three idiots will never end this conversation. I start my engine and went to school.

Chapter Six

A shton POV

    I arrive in school and I quickly made my way out in my car. I notice people are staring at the same direction even my friends. I follow their gaze and my eyes go wide. It's her the nerd, she's not wearing her signature eyeglasses and jeans with big sweater. She wear white short that visibly shows her flawless long white legs and black simple shirt but looks so sexy on her. She let her long straight hair down and when she walk it bounce and shine because it illuminate the sun light. But she seem to be oblivious to her sorrounding and keep walking.

"Hey! What happen to the nerd? She's freaking flawless man!" Xander said

"Look at that butt! Fuck she so sexy!" Ethan add

"Will she look new to me. Especially her eyes, look how mesmerizing it is!" Lucas said

"Shut up ok!" I said I don't know but I don't like the way they describe her. I feel pang in my chest that I don't want others to see her looking like that. It's bothering me.

"Babe!" Ellie greet me with a hug and I avoid her arms. I head to my first class and thankfully nerd and I have same first class. I sit beside her but she did not notice her. I stare at her and I bend down so I can see what she up to. She's reading a book what a good girl before I could pull my head I inhale her scent, not as the same scent I smell from those sluts in school but a very sweet like strawberry scent. She look at me and her eyes almost pope out.

"Hi!" I said while I pull out myself to her.

"What are you doing here?" She asked me confused

"What are you talking about it's my class here!" I answer her

"But your sitting there?" She said and pointing towards my usual seat.

"Can I not sit here?" I ask her

"No it's ok nobody sitting there anyway!" She said while shaking her head.

"So are you ready to go to cafe together?" I asked her. I just want to know what she feel. But before she could answer me. Our teacher came inside and I sigh so much for good timing she have.

"Good morning!" She said. "Have you prepare your short quiz for today?" She asked the class

"No!!!!" The class said together

"Well whether you are prepare or not I will going to have our first quiz. We already delay it last time since I give you a chance to study! It's not my fault that you did not study your lesson last night!" The teacher said.

I facepalm since I did not able to study last night. Though I can 100%0sure that I can answer some questions but not 100% correct. I look at the nerd beside me she's too relax and waiting for the teacher to pass the test paper.

I look at the test paper in my hand and I could only say good luck to me. I notice the nerd beside just simply bend down her head and keep writing. After 10 minutes she raise her pen and paper meaning she's finish.

The teacher collect her paper and told her she can go outside. All of us look at her disbelief! How can she easily answer the question in just very short span of time. She's a nerd, she's genius what can you expect.

I glance outside and I can see her friend jasmine waiting for her. She went out and jasmine drag her while they keep talking. Boys eyeing her from head to toe since she's so sexy and beautiful in her clothes today.

"Ashton eyes on the paper not outside!" Teacher Gisele said

After a matter of 40 minutes I finish my test. I know I will only get half of score. Haizt! My dad will skin me alive if he knows I slack off again.

The bell ring and I went outside. I head to the cafeteria to eat my lunch with my friends. I spot the nerd with her friend whose on their own world talking to each other. They keep giggling and laughing. After ordering their food they sit in the corner side of the cafeteria.

"Ashy.....!" Elli shout loudly and grab all the attention in cafeteria. I cringe of what she name me.

"How many times I need to tell never call me that name!" I said annoyed to her

"Come on babe! I'm sorry!" She said then she link her hands on my arms and quickly swat it.

"Babe!" She whine

I didn't bother to answer her and just left her there. She's so annoying and I hate it when a girl force herself to a guy.

I sit on my usual seat with my friends who are now busy eating their lunch too. I scowl when I feel Ellie sit next to me.

"Babe can I eat your fries?" She ask

"You already have your own fries? Why bother taking mine?" I said to her while I eye her fries in her plate.

"I didn't mean this fries but the other fries!" She said sexily while lick her lower bottom and bite after. Her hands travel to my thigh and I gasp when she grab my junior down there. I push her hands away immediately.

"Stop it!" I glared at her

"Come on Ellie make Ash eat his meal peacefully! If you want you can grab my fries!" Xander said with a evil grin.

Fuck! This stupid friends of mine and this stupid whore can't tame their own lust.

"Please we're eating ok?" Lucas said in a disapprove mood.

Thank God we share sentiment here.

"Xander if you want to bang don't of it here ok? Do you want us to gag? Your gross man!" Ethan said while he pretend to cover her nose and gag.

"Fine!" Xander surrender thankfully

We silently resume eating our meals together . Then the whore suddenly broke it off.

"Ashy... Do you want to go to my house after class? " She asked me battling her eyelashes

"Ask Xander instead Ellie I think he's interested!" I said in bored tone.

"Why do you keep rejecting me baby? You know I like you right?"she said while she hug her arms to me.

"Look I don't like you and if ever I want to use you I will call you!" I said

She walk out and stomping her feet in defeat. Thank God she understand finally.

Chapter seven

Arabella POV

My last class ended and I swear I am so nervous right now. I quickly went outside and walk to the place where we promise to meet. I sight Ashton is already there waiting for me. He sitting while typing something on his phone. I fake a cough to grab his attention and luckily he turns to me.

"Let's go!" Then he put his phone inside his bag.

We head each other car and he look at me shock.

"No way! We have same car and model but only differ in color!" He look at me dumbfounded

"Yup! It's my dad gift to me last year for my birthday!" I told him

"Wow me too!" He said

"So???" I ask him

"Can we take my car? You know it's awkward to drive separately there!" He explained to me.

"Sure!" I said while I nod my head to him

He's car is clean inside and smells like him very manly. I silently inhale to smell his scent. God I'm such a pervert!

We arrive in the cafe and we sit across each other. I order chocolate fratte and cheesecake both my favorites. I glance at his plate I see chocolate cake cake and cook float.

"So you like cheesecake?" He ask me

"Hmm.. it's sweet and yummy!" I said while I sip the fratte

"Do you have a boyfriend?" He said out of the blue. I almost choked when I sip my fratte of his sudden question.

"No?" I said like it's question

"Thank God! Can I court you?" He said. I swear I almost fall from my seat.

"Why!" I ask him confuse

"Because I like you!" He said again I am shock and speechless. I swallow my own saliva and pay my chest.

"You ok?" He asked me

"Wow! I don't expect you to say that!" I said softly

"Why?" He ask me confused

"Because you Ashton Carter and your popular. Why interested in someone like me? I don't understand!" I said confused

"Because it's you. Your beautiful in your own!" He said swiftly

"But we are not suit to each other. I'm a nerd and your Mr. Soo popular in school!" I said.

"Please trust me I like you... As in I really like you a lot!" He said to me while smiling.

"I'm sorry but I can't I don't want to be center of attention and those girls will kill me alive!" I told him

"Just think of it for a moment ok? I will not force you to answer me right a way! Just give me a chance!" He said trying to convince me

I nodded to him and we eat our food again. After few minutes we finish our food and we went to the nearest park. Ashton makes me sit on swing and slowly push me. He stare at me with a sweet smile on his face

"Hey is their something on my face?" I asked while I wiped the corner of my lips as if theirs something on it

"No silly!" He chuckled to me.

"Ashton your weird!" I told him while I shake my head to him

"Why?" He ask

"Because it's rude to stare like that!" I explained to him

"So, how about I pick you up in your house tomorrow morning so we can go together in school!" He ask me.

I look at him shock, how many times this guy shock me today! My heart can't keep up with his shocking surprises and I swear if I have problem in my heart I will have heart attack at this moment.

"Ummmn.. sorry but I don't think it's a good idea!" I said to him.

"Ok I'm sorry! I just want to get closer to you!" He told me while I feel like he's feeling sorry.

"No! It's about my family! My father and brothers are all overprotective. I don't want you to be grill by them, I swear they all super annoying. My mom is so ok! But the rest they are annoying!" I explained to him

"I thought you don't want to be with me that's why you refuse. Thank God! It's not like that! Well I can understand them, I f I have a sister they will definitely go through me if they want to get her" he said while he look at me seriously.

After that,we talk only random things and we decide to go home. Once I get home my dad and my mom, of course the two idiots are all waiting for me in the living room. My dad stand up and so my mom to greet me and hug me.

"How is it?" My mom asked excitedly

"It's ok mom!" I said. I know it's wrong to hide something to them but right now I feel like it's the right thing to do.

"How's your date!" Dad said while he kiss my forehead.

"It's not a date dad! We just talk that's all. And it's all about our project" I said

"Really?" Daniel said while he look at me

"That's a lame excuse dear sister " emman said and I scowl to him

"Of course not! We're just friends nothing more! We went to cafe to do our project!" I said

"Then why not do it here?" Daniel insist

"So you can grill him? And do something to him?" I hissed at them

"Princess remember this, we love you so much! And we all wanted the best for you. If any one try to take advantage of your kindness and heart they will answer us. You might think we're annoying but we love you. We don't want you to get hurt! Boys are evil!" Dad said and I raise my brow to him

"Boys are evil dad?" I repeat what he said.

"Well except me and your brothers!" Dad said

"Enough! Why can't you leave my sweety alone. Yeah boys are evil your dad once a Playboy so he knows that feeling!" My mom said looking smug at my dad. Serve you right dad!

"Ok I admit I am Playboy back before but when I have your mother. I am the sweetiest, loving, cringy and caring husband in the world. Right honey?" Did said while he hug my mom waist. And kiss her on the lips.

"Mom dad stop that PDA for once. So gross!" Daniel while he snort his nose.

"Dad and mom is my ultimate goal!" Emman said while laughing back

"Haizt! Whatever I got to go to my room now. !" I said and I make my way to my room.

chapter eight

Ashton POV

It's been a month since I started courting her. I never expect this will take long. My friends have been laughing at me since I can't get the nerd say yes to me. And I wonder why? I keep following her everywhere like a lose puppy. I even buy flowers for her everyday. Is it still not enough? How long does this girl take me as her boyfriend.

Right now, we are currently in the library. I stare at her simple face. She never wear makeup, she always go natural and simple.

The bell ring and thank God spending time here in library makes me go crazy. She stand up and I quickly take a step beside her. She glance at me and smile.

"Sorry I know staying here in the library is boring. But I want to answer my assignment ahead." She said . What a good girl how I wish I have same way of thinking like her. But nah! I would never happen.

We went outside the library and head to our next class. It's physical education which I love the most. We went to each respected dressing room, since we need to change for our P.E outfit.

When I went to class, she's already there! I am aware how the girls , look at her and I think they try to bully her. What I admire about her is that she never easily get swayed. She's a nerd but a feisty one.

I sit beside her and smile.

"Hi! You ok?!" I asked her

"Yup!" She said then turn her attention to our teacher whose now discussing something. I tried to listen too.

"Last time, I group you into four groups and made you compete each other. Today I want you to give me a proper insight on what should a team should be. Since I observe the last game you all lacking of it. Give me a short essay about it. After you pass you can go out to class. We will not have any physical interaction!" Our teacher said.

Shit! Essay? I hate it. It's better we play games!

I look at Arabella and she immediately comply what the teacher said. She's writing seriously on the paper without looking up. After a couple of minutes she raise her pen and the teacher collect her paper. She tells her she's dismiss.

She look at me and said.

"You ok?" She asked

"Yup wait for me outside!" I told her then I began scrabbling some letters to write an essay. After awhile, I finished it and I went outside immediately. I look around and I saw her reading some books again.

"Hey!" As I approach her

"Let's grab some snack!" I asked her

She nodded and set aside her book and put it inside her bag. We walk towards our car. She ask me this time she will be the one to drive and we will use her car instead. I agreed and slip inside.

Her car smells like her, strawberry scent and sweet. I notice a big cute stuff toy in the back seat.

"Is that yours?" I asked her while I point the stuff toy.

"Yup my brother Emman always put that in my back seat. It's his gift to me in my birthday. He doesn't want me to leave it in our house" she said while she smile at me widely making her dimple visible.

"You have such sweet, thoughtful, caring brother huh?" I asked her

"Nah... Their too much sometimes, their overprotective! Especially my dad but I love them so much. Sometimes when they're in the house they will sneak into my room and sleep there. They always fight but when it comes to me they will understand each other" she said while she Chuckle remembering her brother.

"I would love to meet your brothers!" Fuck what did I said? This mouth of mine sometimes have his own brain.

"Oh no! That's not a great idea Ashton! My brothers are all crazy, maybe some other time" she said while she shakes her head vigorously. Ok I understand maybe her brother really are scary since she doesn't really want me to meet them.

"We're here!" She exclaimed

Then we went outside her car and enter the cafe that we used to hang out.

"Hi good afternoon, welcome to sweet home cafe. Here's your menu, call me when you want to order" a waitress said while we sit in corner side.

We took the menu and began to select our order. As usual she order chocolate ice cream fratte latti and strawberry cupcake with chocolate on top flavor. This girl really love sweet a lot.

"You really love sweets huh? Especially chocolate!" I said while I grin next to her.

"Who wouldn't? I mean chocolate is the best food in the world. I could go all day for it" she said while I shake my head and chuckled to her answer.

"So! I will buy you hundreds of chocolate of you make me you boyfriend" I smiled wickedly to her.

"Ashton are you sure about this?" She asked me

"Yup never been this sure" since Xander Birthday is coming I need to make you as my girlfriend as soon as possible. I can't lose to a bet. I added to myself.

"But I think we're not belong to each other. Just look at me and you. I still can't believe even now that your courting me what more being my boyfriend!" She said softly.

"No it's doesn't matter to me. What I want is you and me. Just because your a nerd and I am popular we're not meant to be!?" I said like I am being hurt.

"Ashton, are you really serious?" She asked me

"Yes very serious!" I answered her

"Then I want to be your girlfriend too. I don't have any of experience in dating" she said shyly

"That's ok we will take it slow. Promise you will not regret it" I said... Yes I'm going to win the bet.

"So????..... Is this a yes?" I continue

"Yes!" Then she smile.

Finally!!!!!!!!!!

****

chapter nine

Arabella POV

It's been one month I said yes to Ashton. I still can't believe it, even Jasmine is so shock when she received the news. She even shout out. Elli and Aliyah always make fun of me. They said Ashton and I will not last long.

I just shrugged my shoulder and didn't care. They can't bully me since my dad is a powerful business man. He reprimand the school principal to never let me get bullied by other students.

As if as clue, Aliyah and her group of cheerleaders pass by. I am currently sitting in the bench where we usually meet with Ashton and his friends.

"So princess did your prince charming has still not dump you?" Aliyah said

I just look at her and smile.

"Really? Your pathetic nerd. How could you dream that he is going to love you. One day you will regret this" one of Aliyah minion said

"He's gonna dump you after he gets what he wants from you. Ashton is not a serious type of a guy especially the likes of you? Have you seen yourself in the mirror?" Aliyah said

"Look your nerd, maybe Ashton wanted to taste a nerd. Or perhaps he wants you because of a bet!" Minion said

"Hahahahaha... For sure... I will laugh at you and you will come running crying like a sick puppy. I can't wait for that to happen!" Aliyah said

"I don't know what I done to you. But if that's happened then it's my problem not yours!" I said with chin up.

They all look at me and stomp their way. Thank God those girls are really meanie.

I notice Ashton and his friends on the way to me.

"Let's go!" Ashton said as they arrived next to me

"Can we join you guys?" Lucas said

"Yeah! It's been awhile, we miss hanging out with Ashton. Please Ara?" Xander said while he look likes a puppy in his eyes.

"Back off!" Ashton smack their heads.

"Ouch bro! Your so violent! " Xander said while he scowl at Ashton

"So princess can we come to your date? Pretty please? " Ethan said to me.

I look at Ashton trying to ask help from him.

"I said back off!" Ashton shout out and grab my hands. Then we walk together leaving his three friends.

"Ashton that's rude! Let them come ok? They are your friends!" I said then I glance back at the three still looking at us. Then I signal them to it's ok to come with us. They laugh and grab they're back packs and running to us.

"Thanks princess!" Xander said then he put his arms on my shoulder

"Yup thank you princess. I'm so glad your Ashton girlfriend. You can change his mind. You know his always meanie to us!" Ethan said while he grab my arms and hug it.

"Thank you princess. Welcome to the family!" Lucas said then hug me. My God three boys practically hugging me in the parking area. I look at Ashton whose fuming in anger . He smack the three with his back pack .

"I agree to let you three come, but I did agree to steal my girlfriend. Give her to me before I change my mind and left you three here!" Ashton said and he grab me again.

Then we all went to the usual cafe that we always eat after the class end.

"So princess what's your plan in the future?" Ethan said

"I planning to get medical degree. I want to be like my mom!" I said.

"You want to be a doctor!!! " Xander said.

"Your mom is so hot!" Ethan said while he wink at me

"Tell that to my dad and I swear he will fire you with bombs!" I said while laughing

"Must be hard to have such parents princess?" Lucas said

I shake my head and smile to them

"Nope! My mom and dad never force me anything. Actually it's really my decision to be a doctor. I used to see my mom savings life. I thought it's so cool!" While I giggle in front of them. I take off my eyeglasses since my eyes gets itchy. I notice they all look at me rather staring at me.

"Do I have something on my face?" I asked them eyeing the three of them

"Your beautiful!" Xander broke the silence.

"Shout up!" Ashton said then he hold my hand and interwine our fingers together.

"About that project tomorrow, my God how can we complete it? That teacher only give us one week to complete. I am not even in the middle of it. How will I finish it tonight!" Lucas said

"Your not finish Lucas?" I asked him

"We all not yet finish princess!" Xander said.

"When did we finished our projects? We always submit late anyway!" Ashton said

"But that bad… How can you pass your senior year then!" I asked them with concerned

"Nah! We always pass princess. Our parents always makes good donation to this school!" Ethan exclaimed

"Let's all finished your projects then!" I said to them. Then they look at me dumbfounded

"Huh?" Xander said

"Lets finish it. We still have time!" I smile to them

"Babe that's ok let this idiots to do their projects, it's their problems" Ashton said then he hug me on my side.

"Bad Ashton!" Ethan said

"No! I am not bad!" Ashton glared at him

"Looks whose talking. I bet your not even starting your project!" Xander scowl at him

"Hey that's enough guys! Come on lets finish your work and stop wasting time" I said while I clap my hand signal them to stop. "So who has loptop with you?" I asked them

They all look at me weirdly and I look at them with wide eyes.

"What?"

"Princess who goes to school with lop top on hand? That's too baggy!" Xander complain

"I can't believe you guys! You need to take some notes you know! " I explained

"Your such a good girl I swear. Your too good for Ashton!" Lucas said

chapter ten

Ashton POV

Two months later....

Having such a good girlfriend influencer in school is a good thing. My friends, together with her always hang out and do our projects and homework. She's very simple and kind hearted. I don't want but I feel guilty about the things we will do to her. I want to tell Xander to stop the bet and just move on. But I can't seem to say to him. I am such a coward.

Just right now, were having our lunch together in the cafeteria. Ara bring her friend Jasmine in out table where I sense that Lucas my friend keeps glancing at her.

"So Ara my birthday is coming next month. I hope you and Jasmine can go together" Xander said while he eye Jasmine.

"I think I pass... I am not into parties" she said shyly.

"Come on! It's only few people" Xander persuade us

"Like whole campus...it's your definition of few people Xander?" Lucas said to him

"Come on dude! I just want Jasmine to have fun. I bet Ashton here will come together with Arabella right?" Xander then turn to me and I feel guilt inside of me. I turn to look to Ara she just smile to me in return.

"I don't know maybe, If she want right babe?" I said while I asked Ara

"Yeah! Anyway next month will be our major exam. I don't want to have poor grades. I need to study Xander" Arabella said to Xander.

I kno she's not a type of girl to walk in a party. She's more on library and dating books or some cafe and eat sweet foods. She just simple kind of girl and I like her that way.

Speaking of her, we never been to first base. We kiss but smack only, I feel guilt when I intimate her. You know about our bet, it's kind of frustrating.

"Ashton...." Xander said while he have this eye signal to me. I just shrugged my shoulder and continued eating my food. While Ara glancing at me.

"What?" I asked her

"You really like fries!" She said then she put more fries in my plate.

"Thanks babe!" Then I smile to her and give her a quick kiss on the lips.

"Gezz get a room you two" Ethan said while he scowl looking to us.

"How about get your own girlfriend!" I said to him while I look to Ara whose red as tomato right now.

I put my arms in her shoulder and whisper to her.

"Let's have a date today?" I said while she look at me blushing. She nodded and I smiled to her.

After our lunch, we went to our respective class. I am excited getting to our date since it will our first going out as couple. Yes! And we never have intimate moment because of this jerks of my so called friends, they always want to tag along with us.

Our class ended and I went to meet Arabella in our usually spot. I spotted her walking towards me.

"Shall we babe?" I asked her and she smile. I interwine our fingers and kiss it.

"Ashyy!" Elli said while she went close to me and gives me a quick kiss on my cheeks. I could sense that Ara is tense.

"What do you want Elli?" I asked her trying to calm my temper. Last thing I want is arguments and I don't want Ara to witness it.

"What did you see to this nerd Ashy? She's very simple and nerd. Your not good for each other" she said while she eyed Arabella in distaste.

"She's my girlfriend accept it already. If you have nothing important to say then I think we better leave" then I lead Ara to parking area and I put her into my passenger seat and I took the driver seat and drive.

As I drive I notice her making glance at me because we already passed in our favorite cafe. She throw me a question look. I grab her hand, hold it and squeeze it while I smile to her.

I stop the car and we went outside.

"Where are we?" She asked me

"It's a secret place... But since you are my favorite girl and my girlfriend I take you here. It's a special place to my family and I hope you will like it" I said and explain

Then I grab her hand and we walk together. We stop in the security and one look of the security to me and he immediately recognize me. He let us pass and enter the gate.

As we came inside, I noticed Ara staring at the sorrounding. Her eyes sparkle and she smile so sweetly.

"Oh my God! What is this place Ashton? It's so beautiful... I never seen this kind of place before" she said while she twirl around she look like a kid that went to amusement park. Her face grace with sparkling eyes and smile.

"It's my family very own park and garden. My mom loves to plant Flowers and this is my father gift to her in their wedding day" I said to her while I put the blanket and basket so we can have picnic.

"Where did you get that?" She asked me implying about the basket and the blanket.

"We have people working in here. They are taking care of the plants and flowers here. Do you like it? Do you want to pick some?" I said to her.

"No! It's beautiful... I still can't believe that this place exist. Your father must have love your mother too much for he gifted her this huge and wonderful garden" she said

"Yup! They love each other and honestly dad has been very busy but my mom always understand him. I don't know but I can't help to wonder how does our life turns out if he doesn't have company to run" I said while I look into the sorrounding

"Ashton don't say that! Your dad must be busy but he loves you and your mom. He will never work to his fullest if he don't love you both. He just wanted to give the best and everything to you and your mom" she said to me while she sit next and hug me at the side.

"How can you say such a thing? Your born to have your parents attention drown to you since your only one daughter" I said while I caress her cheeks

"Oh! Yes I am their princess, they always said that! And I love it how they love me and the attention they all give me. But Ashton with or without attention our parents love us so much. Don't think of anything else" she said to me.

How can I get to lucky to have such good and amazing girlfriend. She never think negative at all. She always appreciate things in a good way.

I bend down my head and capture her lips to mine. At first she's taking a back and I feel her tense. But little as the kiss turns to passionate and hot she return my kiss and she put her hands in the back of my neck. I bit her lips, making her moan and I push my tongue inside her as I tasted her sweet and delicate mouth just the way I imagine it would be.

I slowly let go of her, as we parted, we breath heavily and both of us try to catch our breath. I look at her but she look down and her cheeks is so red.

"Hey what happen?" I asked her

"I don't think you don't like the way I responded to your kissed. I don't have any experience and it's my first time" she said shyly and she blush even more. I chuckle while I look at her amuse.

"Hey! It's not about how you response, it's about how we feel. Do you feel this?" I took her hand and put it in my chest. She look at me confused. "It's beating to hard and loud it's because of what I feel for you" I told her with loving eyes.

"I feel the same way too Ashton!" She said while she keep blushing.

"Hey you are so red, you better be get used to it since I am planning to do it more" I said while I wink at her. Her eyes turns wide and she smile to me.

"Don't tease me Ashton!" She said

"I am not! I like so much. Thank you for being my girlfriend!" I said then I captured her lips once again till ne ran out of breath.

Chapter eleven

Arabella POV

The dated with Ashton in their private garden is one of the most amazing day of my life. I will never regret I gave him my first kiss and I think I am falling in love of him. I really don't know if it's good or bad since I never heard him said I love you to me. I guess I just need to keep my feelings since I don't want to scare him. I love how our relationship grow and I don't want to rush it just because of what I feel.

I brush my teeth and comb my long black hair as I look at myself in the mirror. I dress in casual today since mom asked me to accompany her in the hospital and after that we will go mall and go shopping. Dad is so persistent that he will come with us but mom said that it's mother and daughter bonding time which makes my dad silent. I love how my dad is so whipped against my mom.

After I finish grooming myself and I went downstairs. I saw my mom, dad and of course, my brothers Emman and Daniel. They all turn to me when they notice me.

"Wow sis! You look different!" Daniel said

"She's always beautiful, she's my daughter after all!" My dad said and kiss me my forehead

"Aww honey! Come on let her go and so we can go and boys please I swear if I smell girls in my sofa. I will both kill you!" My mom said to my brothers.

My brothers are all Playboys. When mom and dad are not around in the house sometimes they bring their girlfriends. I swear I really wanted to throw up cause those girls are so naughty and they all scream sex.

Mom and me went to her car. But dad stop us before we can get in.

"Ladies I will drive you to your destination!" Dad said while he look at my mom

"Archer I swear, we can go alone together ok?" Mom said

"Honey, you both are my queen and princess they're is no way I will not drive you. Come on text me if you are finished then I will get and drive you to wherever you want!" My dad said

"How about your work honey!" Mom said then she put her hands to my dad shoulder

"Work is work.. but you both are my life. Please honey!" He said

"Mom just let dad drive us. You know dad after the hospital we will go to mall, it will be burden and hassle to you" I told my dad

"Princess how could you say such a word" my dad said in horror. "You both will never be burden or hassle to me. In fact I will b delighted and happy to serve my queen and princess" he said to us lovingly.

"I swear dad your so cheesey, no wonder mom falls for you!" I said then I get into his car without waiting for them since I can feel they need their moment together. Turns out I am right, dad kiss my mom in the middle of our parking area and with many bodyguards around us. I shake my head and focus my attention to my phone.

I notice I have new message and open it. It's from Ashton greeting me good morning.

"Morning too babe! Did you just wake up now?" I press send

My phone beep after five minutes. I glance at my parents who are still being lovey dovey. Then I read Ashton message.

"Yes just woke up babe! How are you?" Ashton said

"Hmm.. I'm going out with my mom" I type and send.

"Oh mother and daughter date babe? Good for you. My dad asked me to go with him in the company. He want to train me early since I am the only one heir of his empire"Ashton reply.

"Hahahah... I will go with mom in the hospital too. Though she will not train me but I love to go there since my mom is my ultimate role model. I want to be just like her, a well known doctor is what I want to be" I type the message and press send again.

"Wow! Future doctor huh? You don't want to be one your dad CEO in his empire?" Ashton reply after five minutes again.

"Nope! I leave it to my brothers! I think taking care of people is what my heart desire and mom said I should go for it" then I send it to Ashton.

"Good for you! By the way I need to go to bathroom and take a bath. Want to see me I'm the shower babe?" As I read Ashton message my cheeks immediately heated. This is pure torture.

Then a playful idea pops out in my mind. I scroll my phone gallery and I search my selfie photos where I think I look good. After series of debating to myself to what pictures I will send to him. I just decide to pick the picture I took this morning before I went downstairs. It's my out fit for today.

A "ding" sound I heard after 2 minutes.

"What the fuck are you wearing?" Ashton message in my phone.

"A clothes!" I reply

"Fuck! Cover your chest ok.. secure you blazer just don't open it too much. My God! Don't you ever wear something like that in school or I swear I'm gonna kill anyone looking at you" Ashton message to me in my phone

"Silly I'm with my mom!" I text

"So? What makes you think guys will not ogling at you if your mom is around?"he said

"Ashton it's just a clothes ok? I also wear blazer to cover my expose body"

"What did you decide to wear that anyway? I never seen you like that!"

" Hmm.. I am always like this it's just that I don't want to be center of attention. I want to stay away from trouble especially guys... You know my brothers will break lose of they know I have boyfriend, so I just want to be nerd and anyway I am comfortable wearing nerds clothes"

"I think I will go to nerd clothes so that nobody will steal you away from me" Ashton reply to my text

"As if!"

"Babe I know beyond that nerd look, their someone whose beautiful, gorgeous and sexy in that nerd body. First time I saw you and you drop your eyeglasses and I noticed your eyes it's beautiful like emerald gem. I swear I never been so attracted to any woman in the past, it's just you!"

"Hahahah.. flattery will get you nowhere Ashton!" I reply to him

"Who knows babe.. "

"Hey what are you laughing there?" My mom said. I never notice they are both in the car.

"Nothing mom!" I reply

"Really? Is that one of your suitors?" Mom said teasingly

"Nope mom!" I whine

"Princess no boys please.... I don't one to kill someone" dad said dramatically

"Daddy... You will always be my prince charming you know that!"

"Glad to hear that baby!" He said then he kiss my forehead

"Daddy don't call me baby please? " I pout to him

"Honey... It's waste of time convincing your dad, you know him. He will always see you as his baby!" My mom chuckle

"But I am the oldest mom. Those stupid boys should be the baby not me" I complain

"Your my one and only girl princess, so therefore you are my baby!" My dad said in a final tone. I just close my eyes and sigh. I will never win this kind of arguments because my family always see me as their baby.

Chapter twelve

A shton POV

After series of debate between my father and I about me attending the gala for tomorrow, he once again force me to attend the gala tomorrow night which I really hate. I would rather watch Netflix or play billiards in Xander or Ethan house that talking to those businessman.

My dad wants me expose as early as possible since he said I badly need to recognize the people that surround the business world. It will be great that I will knew them in a early time.

I am currently in the mall, precisely in Armani. I look over to each suits that will enhance my interest then I decided to go over a simple gray one.

My phone beeps when I come to sit in the driver seat. I open the message and it was Arabella, my beautiful girlfriend.

I decided to call her and I dial her number. It takes three rings for her to answer.

"Ashton...!" She said in whispered

"Why are you whispering babe?" I asked her.

"Nothing! Why did you call?" She asked me still whispering

"Hmm.. you message me and I decided to call rather than messaging it's more convenient this way" I explained to her.

"Uh uh I get it! Where are you?"

"Parking lot of a mall. My dad wants me to attend the gala tonight, so I went to the mall to buy my suit for tonight"

"Your going to attend too?"

"Too? Means your going?" I said in shock

"Yup, my whole family rather! My dad always brings us to the gala or any charity" she said.

"So I guess we're going to see each other tonight?"

"Yup!"

Then I heard something in her background.

"Princess what are you doing?" A male voice asked.

"Dad I am talking to a friend" Arabella said.

So that's his dad.

"Princess are you sure you want to come tonight? You don't want parties! But don't worry the boys and your mom and I are going to be there ." A male voice with a consoling sound.

"Dad I'll be ok, don't worry! I. Not a child" she whined

"Oh your not a child but your a baby!" A teasing tone of a male voice.

"Hahaha.. baby.. come" another male voice in the background

"Dad they're teasing me again. I told you never called me that again. These idiots will just keep teasing me" she whine. Aww.. her whine voice sound so cute.

"Daniel, Emman stop teasing your sister" their dad voice

"Boys I swear if you keep teasing your sister i am going to ground you" a voice of a female

"Serve you right you two idiots" Arabella burst laughing.

"Dad she call us idiots, this little sister of mine"

"What little sister? Hey I am older in one year to both of you. Why are you keep acting like I am the younger one here? You little boys!"

"Dad this little sister of ours is such a bully?" Her brother said

"Stop dad! Get these two idiots mom, they're so heavy. Get off you brute! You smell girls again" hahahaha what a family she have

"Well it's not our fault girls falls over us little sissy"

"Hahaha... Are you jealous? Aww your such a baby. Come let us hug you. You will always be our favorite girl you silly!" Then I hear her screaming again

"Stop stop! Idiots... Idiots.. stop pestering me for god sick" she huff.

"Ok that's enough boys. Why don't you get ready for the gala tonight?" Her mom said

"Done mom!"

"Me too"

"How about you sweetie?" Her mom asked her

"I'm done too!"

"Let us see... " Her brother ask

"Why?"

"Who knows what kind of dress you will wear. We better check it first. We don't want boys ogling at you" her other brother said

"Mom I swear! If these two boys will not go out from my room this instant, I'm gonna throw them in my window " she hissed

"Princess ok! That's enough boys! Don't make our princess mad, right baby?"

"Dad!!!! Not again!" She whine

Then I heard a footstep getting far.

"Hello are you still there?" She asked me over the phone.

"Yup baby"

"Oh God you heard everything?"

"Yes! Your their baby huh?" Then I chuckled

"Ashton it's not funny! I swear my family is crazy. Especially my brothers" she hissed angrily

"I think they love you so much. I can sense even I am just listening. They are protective to you cause they love you" I said to her truthfully

"Nah! Overprotective that's the right definition of it. Anyway I need to hang up I need to get ready for the party tonight. See you there Ashton!" She said

"Yes princess see you! Bye!" Then I cut the call bottom.

Then I drive off to my house. My mom and dad are already preparing for the party.

****

After a few hours later.....

My parents and I drove to the reception of the gala. Of course a lot of popular people, rich, politicians and businessman are all gather together.

I look into the crowd, hoping to see Arabella but I think they not yet arrive. Then dad introduce me to his co businessman. I introduce myself and greeted them.

Then all the sudden the crown eyes look into the entrance. I saw Arabella parents, brothers and her. She look sexy and you can't trace any single look of a nerd in her. She can even distinguish as model because she so sexy and beautiful.

Then they walk into our direction and our eyes meet. I smile towards her and she respond in same.

"Martin and family... Still looking handsome as ever" my dad greet Arabella father.

"Carter, thank you! Yours too. You have a wonderful family" he said while his arms around his wife. While his sons arms are all over Arabella arms.

"By the way this is my one and only son, Ashton" my dad introduce me to them.

"Hello sir" then I shake his hand.

"Oh theses are my family, my two sons Daniel and Emman, my daughter Arabella and of course my lovely wife Ysabella" her dad introduce them.

My dad and Mr Martin have a talked about business. Arabella and her brothers are now talking sitting in the table. I can see her giggle when her brothers whisper something on her. I wish I could stay beside her.

Chapter thirteen

Arabella POV

Ashton and I are getting close after series of date we had this past few days. After the gala, he said he wants to get closer to me and want me to introduce h to my family, which I disagree. I told him, I will tell my family at the right time.

Thank God he understood

A pair of arms pull me off from my thoughts and I look at the person whose responsible of it. Of course it's none other than my boyfriend Ashton.

"Babe!" He said while he enveloped me in his arms and took a quick kiss in my lips.

"Ashton where in the school campus" I glared at him. I mean I am not used to him getting intimate around many people.

"Babe it's normal! Anyway why can't I kiss my beautiful girlfriend?" He said in whine time and he began to nozzle his nose to my hair.

"Ashton other students are all looking" I hissed at him while I try to pry my body to his hold. But the guy didn't budge at all and still continue his assault.

"Babe didn't I tell not to dress clothes that will attract other boys?" He then scan me from head to toe. The thing is he doesn't want me to wear clothes that will appealing to other guys, he want me to remain my clothes as nerd.

"Let's go and let's change your upper" He said then grab my hand and drag me to the nearest restroom.

"I don't have spare shirt Ashton" I said while I eyed my clothes. I think it's ok, I am just wearing jeans with sleep slightly crop long sweater. Though it reveals some small parts of my tummy when I lift my hands. Other than that, I can't see any wrong.

"Wait here!" He said then he went to the direction of our school locker. Then he came back with a white shirt on his hand.

"Wear this" He said and he usher me to go inside the restroom and change. I sigh and just obey him.

After I change I came out and he look at me. He smile and made a hand approved gestured.

"So can we go to cafeteria? I think i am very hungry" I asked him them he smile and kiss me lovingly in my lips.

"Your wish is my command!" He said. Then he held my hand and we went to cafeteria.

Everyone in the cafeteria snap their heads to us when we enter the door. I consciously look around and try to loosen Ashton arms on my shoulder. But he look at me and glared.

We sat on our usual spot, and as usual his friends are all present.

"So you guys seem getting closer huh?" Ethan greeted us with a playful grin.

"Shout up!" Ashton said to him.

"Ashton so my birthday party will be next. I think you did not forget about it right?" Xander said while Ashton glared at him. I just shrugged at their conversation.

"So will you come Arabella? Please? Ashton will come anyway! Right Ashton?" Xander said while he give me his puppy look.

"I think I can come.. " I said to him finally. He's been convincing me to come to his party and I don't know why.

"You will come?" Ashton look at me suprise

"Yup!" I said to him and he nodded to me.

After that, I felt something is off. It's like Ashton is not his mind, he seem to be drifted away in his thoughts.

"You ok babe?" As I put my hand in his forehead.

"I'm ok babe!" He said as he took my hand and hold it. "Let's go!" He said to me. After we finished eating our food.

He took me to my class since we have different class.

"Bye see you after this!" I said to him as I enter my classroom

"Hmm!" He nodded and went away to his class. Good thing our classroom is just near.

Our teacher seem to be late and I decided to read my book since I have nothing to do. I didn't notice Ellie and Aliyah towering me in my desk.

"Enjoy it nerd while you still have the chance. But once his done with you, he will throw you like garbage since you meant to be there anyway" Aliyah said while her eyes fired up towards me.

" Your such a bitch, you think Ashton really loves you? I bet you are a virgin and he just wanted you to spread your legs for him and once he get it, he will no longer need you. He will come back to us since we know how to please him!" Ellie said

"I don't know what are you talking about. But if you have something against me and Ashton talk to him!" I said while I still reading my book pretending that I am affected by their harsh comments.

"Bitch!" They both said as they went to their seat since our teacher has arrived. Thank God!

After the class ended I literally run out the classroom since I don't want to meet with those girls again. I went to Ashton class, and I saw him talking to a chicks who looks like flirting with him. I bit my lower lips and think positive. Ashton will never do that to me.

Ashton saw me in the entrance and he made his way to me.

"Hey did you wait long here?" He asked me while checking me.

"Nope just finished my class!" I lied to him and I smile

Then he held my hand as went to out next class. Till our all class ended and we went home.

Right now I am in my bed ready to sleep but my thought has linger to what Ellie and Aliyah said.

"Is he just playing me?" I asked myself

I shake my head and try to divert my mind to other things. But I can't never seem to get off the sight of Ashton and the girls awhile ago. They seem very close and Ashton did not swat her hands as she flirted him.

"Why?" That's the last word I came up and I went to Dreamland.

Chapter fourteenth

Arabella POV

Weeks pass and right now I am preparing myself for Xander birthday party. I told my mom that Jasmine and I will have study session together in her house and we're going to have sleep over there. My brothers are even drive me to Jasmine house to check if I really go there. Those boys I swear!

"You look beautiful and sexy Ara!" Jasmine said as she finished applying me make up.

I look myself in the mirror and I smile. Yup I look good, I can't even hardly recognize myself.

"Let's go, I think we're going to get late!" Jasmine said.

I grab my blazer and put it in my back since cold. I am not usually dress like this. But I want to impress Ashton. Honestly, I get insecure when I saw him last time with that girl. She's very attractive and sexy. That's why I tried my best tonight to look sexy so Ashton will only look at me not other girls. I think I am getting clingy girlfriend.

I drove my car to Xander house since they already texted the location. As I park my car, I noticed many girls and boys making out in the corner. The loud sound can be heard and of course the smell of alcohol is intoxicating.

I cringe as I we walk inside the house. I scan the crown and I look for a sign of Ashton. I jump in shock when I felt an arms in circling me.

"Baby!" I don't have to turn around since I recognize that voice and his perfume too.

"Ashton!" As I turn and smile to him

"You look beautiful babe!" He said while he eyes me sexily.

I didn't see Jasmine maybe she went for a drinks.

Ashton grab my hands and held it. We guide me upstairs and we went inside the room. As the door close , Ashton lounge himself to me and kiss me hungrily.

Soon it became passionate and I can feel his hand caressing my body. He keep kissing my lips till it landed on my neck, he lick and bite my weak spot. I moan his name when his hand went to my zipper and push it down.

I don't know what happen till I can feel I am fully naked in front of him. He lay me down to the bed and he hover over me while kissing and nipping each part of my body.

(Sorry can't continue... Heheheh... But you guys can imagine what happen next... You know..).

After we made love two times, we drifted to sleep. But I woke up since the shouting and loud sound keeps buzzing so I can't sleep well. I turn my attention to Ashton whose sleeping like a baby in my side. I blush as I recall the early thing happen. I just gave my virginity to him. I hope he doesn't see me cheap or whatever. Everyone does that right?

I took out my phone and message Jasmine where is she now. I quickly went to downstairs since she did not reply me back. And I don't want anything happen to her.

I scan the crowd and I saw people gather around the sofa. I think girls and boys having each partner since I can see they are all barely naked.

"So Ashton just made Arabella his girlfriend for a bet?" A familiar female voice I heard.

"Yes! He wants my car and I think I am lose since we saw him taking Arabella in my room awhile ago. I bet he already took his virginity!" Xander laugh

My eyes slowly form tears and a sob escape in my mouth. They all turn to me.

"Wow! Look whose here?" Aliyah said

"See what we told you?"

"Your just a bet!"

"Xander please explain to me, is it true?" I said while my eyes can't stop crying.

"Yes! Ashton and I made a bet. He will make you his girlfriend and take your virginity on the night of my birthday party!" Xander said laughing.

"Xander!" Lukas said angrily

"How dare you?" Ethan lounge at him

"Did you both know about this?" I asked them and they stop their track and look at me.

They look down and I know I don't have to know their answer since it's obvious.

"Hey what happened here?" Ashton voice said.

I turn around and he saw me, he look shock.

"Why are you crying babe?" He immediately went to my side .

"Ashy you don't have to put an act, we already knew" Ellie said

"What?" Ashton said confused

"About the bet baby! You are really one naughty guy!" Then Aliyah kiss me in the lips while shock visible in his face. He look at me worried.

"Babe let me explain!" He said while he try to grab my hand

"Ashton is it true?" I asked him softly while I try not to burst crying.

"Ye..as!...but!" Before he can finish his sentence I strode outside the house without bothering to look back. My hands are shaking as I put the key to my car. I drive my car without bothering to look even Ashton keep banging my car window.

As I drove I park my car in the side. I cried and cried. I don't know what to do since it's my first time. Maybe I get punished for lying to my family. I should have listened to my father and my brothers.

I cried my first heartbreak till I dont have any tears left. I decided to forget everything. I promise myself that this will be the last and first I will cry for love. I don't want to love anymore. I will listen to my father and brothers for now on.

Chapter fifteen

Ashton POV

Five years later.....

The memories of that horrible night appears on my dream again. It became my nightmare ever since it happened. The pain and sorrow that I can see Arabella eyes on that night keeps haunting me.

After that night, I drove to my house and never bother to talk to anyone. I messaged and call her phone hundred times but she never pick up nor reply to my text. I cried as I recall the memories we had that night as we made love.

Monday comes and I hurriedly went to school, hoping I can see and talked to her. Since I know she doesn't skip school and she can't escape me there. I park my car and look around the campus. Her car was not in the parking area yet so I decided to wait there.

I patiently waited till the bell rang. I frown, Arabella never late. So I ran to her class but she's not yet there. I sigh and decided to just sit in the bench where we usually sit together.

"Hey!" Ethan voice

"You ok?" Lucas said

I didn't bother to reply to them. I am still angry to them since they did not try to clarify Ara about it. Especially that Xander I will never forgive him.

"Bro I'm sorry... I'm drunk!....." But before he could finish my fist land on his face.

"Don't you dare say your sorry! Before the party I already told you, I back out. I don't want to do it anymore" I shout to him.

"But you just blurted out and everyone, everybody knows about it since you can't keep your mouth shut!" I said angrily.

"Pray that Arabella will forgive me if not, I can't guarantee I can see you as my friend!" I said then I walked away from them.

Days past by and I worried why she didn't show up in school so I went to the registrar's office. And they said Arabella no longer a student in our school.

I felt like my whole world crush and my heart stop beating. How can I fix this?

I hurriedly went to her resident even though I don't know what will happen to me. But I really need to see her. I need to clarify and clear things to her. I need to tell her something important.

As I spoke to the guard he said the Martin's family no longer stay in the house, they move out yesterday.

Pain... Shock... Infuse me. My whole world is breaking and I can feel my heart break into pieces.

I did not had a chance to say I love her... She left me...

She left me without saying a word.

Five years, it's been fucking five years but my heart still longing to see her. My heart never stop loving her. I have picture of her in my room those times when were together.

I wish I could turn back the hands of time and I can re do my mistake. The woman I love leave me cause I am asshole and jerk.

I know I don't deserve her after all I've done.

I look at her picture and stared at it.

"Where are you? Do you miss me? Did you forget me? " Those are words I wanted to say to her.

Even though I never seen her for five years but it seem my love for her keeps getting stronger. I tried to buried myself in work but I failed. I will always remember her.

Her smile, her giggle and of course her smell is what I been looking for.

I decided to go home and I told my assistant to my prepare my car since I wanted to go home. I hired an agents to investigate about her. But her father hide her perfectly. She seem to be out of touch. Even a picture of her with her family I can't see it. It's like she never exist.

I went to my car and drive off to my house since I feel like I wanted to drink. As I drove I didn't notice a car collide me making our car bump together.

Shit!

After that I lose my consciousness.

I heard a beep sound and some people whispering. I try to open my eyes and I saw white ceiling and smell of hospital greeted me.

"The patient getting conscious now doc!" I heard one said.

My vision became blurry and the words they said echoed in my head.

A woman with white coat hover me and scan my eyes. I think she's my doctor.

As I a about to lose my entire consciousness, a voice that sound familiar to me keeps me going.

"Mom what happened here?" She said then she scan my body and went to my face.

A beautiful pair of green eyes meet mine as shock register in here eyes.

Arabella is now standing in front of me.

Before I could close my eyes , I smile to her.

Am I in heaven? I asked myself

Or she's back?

Chapter sixteenth

Arabella POV

I stared at the person body lying in front of me. I can still feel my body shiver, he still have effect on me. No matter what I try to forget him but I know I failed miserablely. But they're is no way, things will be the same again. I had made a promise to myself after that night.

After crying like million times, I went straight to my home. Yes! Thank God my parents and brothers are all sleeping they didn't witness how devastated I am.

That morning, before my brothers woke up. I went to my parents room. I knock then I peep my head to the door.

"Mom?" I called out my mom.

"Yes sweetie?" My mom said softly I can see still wrap around the blanket and my dad on her side hugging her. My dad stirred and open his eyes.

"Princess what happened? Do you need something?" My dad asked while he get up on my mom side.

I walked inside their room and I swung my body to my mom side. I hug her, as I try not to sob.

"What happened?" Mom said worriedly

"Dad, mom can I transfer school? Or better can we transfer to other place?" I asked them while I can't hold my tears anymore.

"Princess did someone hurt you?" My dad asked me softly though I can sense anger on his tone.

"No dad!" I said while I am still crying.

"Who made you cried then?" Dad said. "Tell me now, I will make them pay for making you cry!" My dad now semi shouting.

"Dad!!!! It's nothing, please!" As I hug my mom again.

My mom look at me and just wipe my tears that falls down to my cheeks.

I heard a footsteps coming close to the room. Then my parents room door open and revealed my two brothers.

"What happened?" Daniel asked

"Mom something wrong?" Emman said

"Your sister is crying, for God sake. Who made you cry Arabella?" My dad now shouting. I know he is serious now since he called my name this time, no endearments anymore.

My brothers came closer and try to make me stand up but I remain frozed in my mom.

"Who did this to you?" Daniel said. I glanced at him and I saw fury in his eyes.

"Name Arabella who dare to hurt you?" Emman said behind him.

"Knock it off guys, I just want to transfer school. I am not happy there" I said while I try to wiped my tears.

"Then why are you crying?" Daniel said

"We will go to your school and asked. Or you better tell us what happened? You won't like the consequences Arabella?" Emman said.

I swear even though they are my younger brother but they are more scary than me when they are angry.

"I will tell you guys, but pleased I don't want anything to happen. Please promise me that you will just transfer me to other place and school. Please dad?" I look up and stared at my dad who is now looking at me

"Honey! If that's what you want! Just tell us why?" My mom said this time. "I promise!" She said while she smile.

Then I narrate the story how I meet Ashton and what happened. But excluded the part about the sex in the party. And I never name anyone. I don't even tell them about who is my boyfriend.

"They made a bet to you? Just because you are a nerd? I will crushed that guy! Tell me the names now!!!" My dad demand

I just stayed frozed in my mom's embraced. She caress my back since I don't have plan to tell them whose involved. Just want to move on.

"Arabella names now!" Daniel shouted at me

"Let's go to her school!" Emman said.

I got up and ran into them before they could go outside the room. I hugged them both and cried.

"Please no, it's my faulted anyway! I lied to you all. Please I'm sorry Dan, Em and dad for not listening to you. Just please don't go there. Can we just moved out and forget it. Please???" I sob

Daniel and emman hugged me tight.

"Do you think it's not pain to us to see you like this? We need to atleast make them pay for what they done to you!" Daniel said while he still hugged me.

"No! I promise I will listen to you... No more boys" I hug them.

"Whoever that guy I will kill him of I know who he is. Seeing you like this, it kills us. We loved you so much more than anything Bella!" Daniel kissed my forehead.

I am so lucky to have them. My parents join them and hug me.

"That's enough, come sweetie. Let's talked. Boys respect her decision, time will come she will tell us right sweetie?" My mom said.

"But mom..." Daniel protest

"Daniel... Respect your sister decision!!" My mom glared to them . I know my mom once she command all of them will follow.

"So what do you want to do sweetie?" My mom caress the strands of my hair that falls on my face.

"Can we transfer please? I promise to be good girl this time!" I plead to her

"You are already good girl. Remember that! It's just people try to take advantage of your kindness. Honey I know how good girl you are because I raised you to be. No matter what happen never be little yourself. You are perfect, beautiful and kind. Whatever they did to you, do not let it get you.

You have us always! We love you more than world" mom said sweetly to me.

I bursted crying into her arms.

"Archer, it's been long since you did not make that cupcake of yours. How about make some to feed our princess here!" My mom said to my dad softly.

"Of course honey!" Dad quietly exited the room.

"You both help your dad!" Mom said to my brothers. They nodded and went to my dad.

"So, you don't have to cry or hide anything to me. You can tell me. I will listen to you and I promise I will never go there or hurt them!" I just love my mom so much. She's my ultimate bestfriend.

I told my mom everything. I even told her the names. After purring all my emotions in my story I feel better.

"You ok? Listen, we will do what you want !" My mom said then hug me. "Let's go before the boys decide to burn the house!" Then mom and I went downstairs only to find my dad and brothers are in trouble in baking.

I hug my dad and brothers.

"I love you so much... Thank you!" They hug me back

"No worries, I'm sorry we did not protect you princess" my dad said and I both kissed them in the cheeks. I grab the mixture in the pan they made and poured to them.

"You little monster!" Daniel said

I run and escape. My mom and dad look at us while we three keep fighting. They tuck me in the floor and tickle me. My laughter boom the entire house since my brothers never stop tickling me.

So lucky to have a family like them. I will never trade them from anything else.

Chapter seventeenth

Ashton POV

A beep sound wakes me up from my deep slumber. I slowly open my eyes and the sight of light almost blinded me. I can feel the side of me moved.

"Oh my God.. honey he's wake up!" I know that voice that's my mom.

"Son! Thank God! I will call the doctor now!" Then dad went outside the room.

"Ashton don't ever scared us like that ever again" mom said while she hug me.

I look over my body and I saw few stitches and bandages. I can't move my left feet when I do it's hurt.

I glance towards the door and I saw my dad and a doctor coming forward to me. I stared at her and I know her. The memory of me lying almost out of conscious that time.

"Where is she?" I asked the doctor. I know her she's Arabella mom, Ysabelle.

"Who!" She whispered softly while she examine me.

"Your daughter.. I saw her with you the last time when I pass out!" I told her.

"Oh my daughter.. she's busy with her patients!" She said to me. I saw how her eyes flakes when she mentioned the word daughter. I bet she knew who I am.

"Can I see her?"

"Your not her patient Mr. Carter but I am! Listen do not look for my daughter!" She said softly I know she warn me.

My parents just listened to us confused.

"Is something wrong?" My dad asked

"Dad , mom can you please get me food, I am hungry please!" I try to dismissed them. Thankfully they agreed.

"I want to talked to her mam!" I said to her.

"Mr. Carter, I don't want to see you near my daughter. The last time I let you near her she cried. We didn't do anything at that time cause she asked us. I don't want any trouble, stay away from my daughter!"

"Mam, I just want to talk to her. I need to see her."

"She doesn't need you. And you don't need her as well. What you need is to recover so I can discharged you out in this hospital" she hissed at me.

"Please mam???" I said while a tears drop in my eyes.

"I don't hold my daughter decision. It's up to her but if I can make decisions for her I don't want her near you" she said then she exited the door.

I called my investigation team and asked them to find Arabella where about. They immediately reply and report said that she's here in the country, working in her mom hospital now.

I smiled as I look into her picture. She's beautiful and sexy, she get rid of her big eyeglasses. She wore white coat just like her mom. I guess she become a doctor just like she told me.

I will get you back....

No matter what happens I will get you...

This time no more bets

No more lies...

I can't wait to have her in my arms again. This time I'll make sure this will last.

I smile creep into my mouth. And I began to plan on what to do. I called my secretary and asked her to deliver flowers in Arabella office.

I need to get strong and recover so I can talk to her and go wherever she is.

I grin as I read the report that she don't have any boyfriend but she have many suitors. To hell with them, I'll make sure they will all dismissed.

She's mine only.

Mine... Mine... Mine..

I will going to have her sooner.

I will going to make her my wife.

Yes!

My wife!

A feeling when you come home and she will be there waiting while she cook dinner for me. She's going to be my home.

Together, we will make a family. I can't wait to have mini Arabella and mini me in the future.

"Ashton honey here are the foods your favorite!" My mom said while she enter the room. Dad tailing her.

"Ashton what does Ysabelle mean a while ago?" Dad asked me.

I told them what happened in the past and they both look at me shocked.

"Are you out of your mind? Good thing the girl didn't asked her father to sue you!" My dad said angrily

"She's kind hearted girl dad. I love her and I want to make her my wife!" I declare to them.

They both look at me shock and their eyes turns wide. Like I said something so impossible.

"Ashton let the girl be! Move on son!" My mother said

"No! I will asked forgiveness to her. I will do anything to make her forgive me mom. Now she's back I will do everything to make her close to me"

"Archer will never allow this Ashton! That guy is ruthless especially when you hurt his only daughter I bet he will going to make you pay this time!" Dad warn me.

"I don't care... I love their daughter and I know she love me too. We cans still be together!" I convinced them

"Ashton son please... Forget her already. They are a lot of woman out there who throw themselves to you. Not her, leave the girl alone son!" My mom said while she hug me.

"Mom for five years, I am waiting for her. Five years of longing and loving her. Did you expect me to just let it go? I been fucking waiting" I hissed

"Son, how about we transfer the headquarters in London? You grandparents are there and I think they missed you so much. We can stay there permanently!"

"Why would I? I won't let her go dad!"

"Ashton our family business and them are already rival please don't put another fued into this." My mom said.

"Then we will merge with them!" I said simply

"What?" My dad look at me like I'm gone crazy

"Merge dad! I am only heir anyway. I own the empire and for the past five years I made it bigger. Since I am the only one heir I can do whatever I want. We will merge we them so no feud will take place" I explained

"I hope it's just simple as that Ashton. Once Archer found out about the bet you done to his daughter he will kill you. Remember that!" Dad said.

"Oh honey... I think we can't change your mind. But son, please love her this time, never break her heart" my mom said.

"Of course mom, you don't have to warn me about it. I intend to keep her forever lock to me this time" I said in final voice.

chapter eighteenth

Arabella POV

My mom told me that Ashton looks for me. So much for being hide for five years huh?

I been hiding for this past five years since I want a fresh start and I want to concentrate on my studies. I took out medical education and finished it. Right now I am one of the doctors of our very own hospital but I still persuade studying since I wanted to be a surgeon just like my mom.

It's been one week since I last saw Ashton after that night I help my mom rescued him. He had a major accident which almost lose his life. Good thing my mom is a good surgeon she able to save him at the right time.

I ran my rounds in the hospital, I am currently in the pathway walking towards the next wards to check out my patients. But as I about to turn around my body bump into something rather someone. I almost lose my footing and I close my eyes as I expect to land my body in the ground but a pair of arms pull me off and supportive me back to stand.

I look to my savior and about to say thank you but I got shock instead. I immediately entangled myself to him and walked out without bothering to say thank you. But he grab my wrist making me stop .

"Hey how are you?" He said while he look at me intensely

"Thank you for saving me back there. I need to go!" Then I pull off my hand to him but he didn't let me go.

"Ara let's talk please?" He plead to me.

"Go back to your room Ashton" I hissed still trying to pull off my hands to him but he still keep it.

"Talk to me please... Look at me" he command but I keep swatting his hands.

"Daniel go to your room. We will talk when you get better ok? I promise!" I said to him.

"Promise???" He said while he stared at me.

"Promise! Then can you go now. I think you remove your IV in no time" I said to him. Thank God this time he let go of my hands.

"Can you come with me? I think I lose my energy" he said .

"I will call nurse for you. You wait!" and about to dial my phone but he took it in my hand.

"No! Please can you come instead? They just keep flirting to me." He whine

"Ashton I don't know about that. Sorry for our nurses acted then but I can't come with you I am not your doctor" I explained to him

"But you own this hospital, you need to take care of me" he exclaimed

"Fine let's go to your room" then he put his arms on my shoulder. I let him since he need to lend on me for support. How did he manage to go down here in his state?

The nurse look at us shocked when they saw us together.

"Doc we're sorry we didn't notice. We are very sorry" they plead.

"That's enough, please get ready his IV. We need to put it again, I will not tell my mom about this. But please be careful next time?" I reprimand them they nodded and head my command.

I took him to his room and help him lay down. I look around and I saw no guardian.

"Where are your guardians?" I asked him while I insert the needle in his veins. Slowly I put his IV again.

"Did replace me for time since I can't work for now. Mom went home to get few things for me!" He said.

"Do not remove it again Ashton, my mom will get mad if she knows it!" I told him

"Oh! Do you have food? I'm so hungry! Please help me?" He said while he scratched the back of his neck.

"You can eat by yourself!" I protest

"Please... I am super hungry. Please" he plead

"Fine" then just in time a food deliver in his room.

I feed him and he eat all the food. No leftovers

"Get rest and I will go now. I need to resume my work now" then I went ahead

"Hey we will talk when I discharge right?" He clarify

"Yes go to sleep!" I said then I close his door.

I inhale as I exited his door. I know it's not right to talk to him again but I want to put things to an end.

I went to the wards where my patients and examine them. I finished all my work exactly three in the afternoon.

As I lean my head on my seat someone knock on my door and I tilt my head to look. "Come in"

My mom grace my room with her white clothes too just like me. Dad and my brothers said like mother like daughter we are because we have the same field of interest.

"Mom" I get up and kiss my mom on the cheeks.

"Sweetie your dad wants us home early. Are you done?" She asked me while she sat on the opposite chair.

"Yes! Just done all my work mom! I am relaxing a bit" I said to her.

"I heard what happen earlier". She told me.

"Yes?" I look up to her to meet her eyes.

"I know it's your life honey! But do you think it's ok to meet him?" She asked me.

"Mom, I can't hide forever. I need to put it an end. I need to forgive him so can fully move on!" I explained to her.

"I know honey, I trust you so much. Anyway that boy keeps bothering me, he wants to know about you!" She said laughing. I look at her and I raised my eyebrows in confusion.

"Why so?" I asked confused

"I don't know but it's up to you sweetie. Whatever decision you will make it's up to you. You grown to be beautiful and wonderful woman and I am proud of that. But I also want you to have time for yourself. After that happened, you closed your door to anyone who try to approach you especially boys. " She said to me.

"Not again mom! I don't want to be in relationship that's why. And I am so fucos in my work and I don't have time to go to dates" I explained while I twirl myself in my seat.

Love is something I don't want for now. I think it's better to be alone and forever single since I am loving it. No commitments, no dates, and no heart breaks.

Chapter nineteenth

Ashton POV

Arabella said we will have a talk when I get better. I am excited for that to happen. Last time when I embrace her, when she bump me and she almost fall in the floor, good thing my reflexes works quickly even though I am sore and pain all over my body because of the accident.

Her sweet gentle strawberry scent hit my nose and believe me I feel like I'm in heaven. The moment I captured her waist and I closed our body together, it's feels so divine. I want to kiss her so badly but no, I don't want to scare her.

Two weeks past and I am thankful that I get discharge from the hospital. Her mom Belle is my doctor and believe me she's the most kind hearted woman, no wonder her daughter takes after her. They have same personalities and the way they treat people.

Archer Martin is a lucky guy and I will be soon since I am going to marry their daughter, Arabella.

"Paul, go ahead of me in the office. I will stop by in my doctor's clinic" I said to dismiss my assistant.

After finished changing my clothes , I went outside and walked over to information area and asked where Arabella office.

I look around and head to her office. I look into bouquet of flowers in my hand while the other hand knock on her door. "Come in"

I went inside and she look shocked, her eyes went wide for a moment. After she recover, she clear her throat and look straight to me.

"What are you doing in here?" She asked while she signal to sit on her sofa.

"This is for you" I give her the flowers and I saw in her case and even on the table have many flowers on it. " A lot of suitors huh?" I eyed the flowers on her room.

"Thank you for this, it's beautiful!" She said then she put it in the case near her.

"I would like to invite you for dinner?" As I sit down and look for the time in my watch and look back again to her.

Then her phone ring and she signal me to wait for a moment.

"Dad!" She greet.

"Hmm.. I don't know maybe I will be late for a little bit. Yes! Tell my brothers to left me some cupcakes of yours. Hahahahah.. yes! Of course dad your cupcakes are the best. Hahahahah... No no.. dad please don't tell mom. Ok bye too Daddy" then she hung up her phone.

She still have sweet family. I smile as I look into her. I noticed how beautiful and sexy she is today.

She's wearing high fitted blue jeans with matching oversized sweater in semi crop. It showcase her bare shoulder and I can say it's fucking sexy especially when she bend down. I could easily spot her inviting cleavage.

She walked towards me and swear I never seen such sexy woman in my entire life. I can almost feel my groin twist, behave my friend please. I pray silently. When she near me I can smell her feminine scent. And I swear I want to kiss her lips pretty badly now. She sit down in opposite of me.

"Why are you here Ashton?" She asked

"I would like invite you for dinner!" I asked her politely.

"Me?" She asked while she point herself. She so cute

"Yup you!" I smile to her.

"I think it's too early for dinner" she look to her watch.

"It's ok, we can go for a walk and talk then we eat our dinner after. What do you say?" I convince her. Then my phone beep, it means I have new message. I read it and it's my mom.

"How about we go to my parents house, they invited me for dinner. I think they will love to meet you!" I said to her with a hopeful smile on my face.

"I don't think it's a good idea Ashton, it's your family dinner. I don't want to intrude" she declined politely.

I shake my head and smile to her.

"Of course not! My mom will be happy of I introduce a girl to them" I encourage her. "Please???" I said in puppy eyes.

"Ashton I can't. Maybe we can have dinner next time and talk but not with your family. That sound personal to you and I don't want to enter your personal life" she said.

I grab her hand and she want to pull off but I hold it still.

"Please... It will make my mother and father happy please please???? Please..." Then I kneel down to her. She gasp and her eyes went wide again.

"Get up Ashton please" She then help me up. But I shake my head.

"Please please... Just this one please!" I almost cried for pleading to her. I hold her hand tightly.

"Fine then we can talk after!" I get up and I shout. "Yes! Thank you... Thank you... Hahahahah... Thank you. Let's go so you can meet my parents. I bet they will going to love you!" I smile cheekily to her.

My heart dance happily just the thought I will introduce her to my parents. I never had any woman I introduce to them, because I know the only woman I want to face my parents is her.

I glance at her as she gracefully took her bag and put the strap on her shoulder but I stop her and took it. She look at me confused and her eyebrows knitted in confusion.

"I will carry your bag for you" I said then I guide her towards the door.

"I can manage Ashton, give me my bag back!" As she try to grab it back. But I dodge her.

"Nope! Come on! I'm famished!"

As went outside, nurses and other hospital employee greeted her. She respond with a genuine smile on her face.

"Hey Ara.. where are you going?" Someone shouted then we both turn around. She look into the person and smile.

"Javier!" Then she ran to him and the guy open his arm for her.

My heart ache of the sight I witnessed. Is he, her lover? But the report said she doesn't have a lover.

"Where are you going?" The guy said after they hug. I balb my feet as I try to suppress my angry and jealousy.

"A friend of mine invited me to dinner " she said smiling to him.

"Really?"he said then she nodded to him. The guy saw me

"Is that him!" He asked

"Yes! Ashton this Javier Knight my childhood friend. Javier this is Ashton Carter" she introduces us. We shake hand and he look at me closely. He gave me a nod and turn to Ara once again.

"I better go, I thought I might ask to dinner too bad I'm late! Hahahah.. but maybe next time!" He said smiling to him

"Yeah next time. We can go with Daniel and Emman" she said.

"Bye Ara, please take care of her" Javier said to me. I nod in response and I grab her wrist, she pull it off but I did not let her. I guide her to my car and help her buckle up her seatbelt.

The drive to my parents house is silent. The only noise you can hear is the a/c and the car engine. I glance to her and I saw her leaning her head on the window while her eyes close.

"You can sleep, I will wake you when we are there!" I said to her.

Then I concentrate myself in driving. While I glance to the woman I love beside me. I need a plan to get her.

chapter twenty

Arabella POV

I don't know if it's right or wrong but I said yes to Ashton when he invited for dinner in his parents house. I hesitated a moment but he's very persistent untill I agreed.

Ashton went inside to a big gate and I saw a beautiful modern house. Their house is so beautiful just like ours, well both family's own hotels chain so I don't wonder why.

He park his car in their garage and I was about to open the door but he stop me. I look at him in confusion.

"What?" I asked him.

"Stay there, I will open the door for you" then he exited in the driver sit and run around on my side to open the passenger door for me. He offer his hand and I took it.

"Thank you!" I said to him then I pry my hand to his since he did not let it go.

"Ashton my hand!" I said to him while we walk towards the entrance of the house. But he just shrugged and keeps walking instead.

I saw his mother and father waiting for us in the entrance. A smile form in their face when they both saw me.

"Oh my God, your bringing a girl at last to meet us" his mother said while she approach us. She kiss his son and hug me. I was taken a back for moment but I regain my compose soon after. I smile to them inwardly.

"Hello, I hope I am not intruding in your family dinner!" I said while I blush since his mom can't keep staring at me.

"Mom don't do that! Ashton said. Thank God he noticed how awkward her mother stares at me.

"Oh I'm so sorry dear! I just surprised and overwhelmed. Your so beautiful and gorgeous no wonder you catch the heart of my son!" His mother said playfully. I avoid their stares since it's so awkward. They must have think that I am his girlfriend.

"Where are your manners, let our soon daughter in-law enter our house honey" his father said.

I look shock and I look to Ashton who seem to ignore his father comment.

I felt his hand guiding me to enter their house. When I am fully enter the house is absolutely beautiful, it's full of modern design.

I took a sit in the living room as his mother seated next to me.

" What kind of food do you like? I hope you will love my cook, I personally cook it myself. Actually I don't do the family business I leave it to my husband and son. Hehehe.. I want to be full time mom!" She said laughing.

"That's good of you Mrs. Carter!" I said politely.

"Don't call me that dear… Call me Sofia or mom instead" she said smiling.

The house keeper said that dinner is ready and we went to dining room.

Ashton and I sitted beside each other while his father and mother sitted on the other side.

"So what do you do dear?" His mother asked me.

"I'm a doctor Sofia". I said then she and her husband look each other.

"So you take after your mom?" His father said.

"Yeah! But it's my dream to be a doctor ever since I am young. With the help of influence too with my mother, I admire her dedication to her work" I said to them.

"Your father already stop working right?" His dad said

"Yes! He wants to have time with my mom together. Actually as we speak they're already on their vacation" I told them as I giggled.

"So who manage both of the business?" His dad asked once again.

"For my dad's business of course it's my brother's and for the hospital, I managed it together with Aunt Emma daughter Emmie"

"Dad stop that! Your talking about business" Ashton said.

" Ashton here is the only son, so he manage alone" his father continue his charade about business.

"Where did you study dear in college? I didn't seen you" his father asked again.

I felt Ashton tense body beside me and i try to avoid his gaze since I know he's looking at me now.

"Actually I went to University of Oxford in United kingdom" I answered to them.

"Oh that's why I didn't notice you. Why not Harvard dear? It's more prestigious than Oxford and best in medical school too!" He inquired

"Actually, I was being recruit to that school but I declined. I wanted to stay away from my home land at that time. I wanted to start a fresh" I said while my hands are sweating due to intense feeling I feel for being hot seat in the dinner.

"Do you cook dear?"his mother asked

"Yes Sofia!" I smile while I try to swallow the food in my mouth.

I felt Ashton squeeze my thighs and I look at him. He smile to me sweetly.

"Mom actually she's good at everything!" He said proudly to his parents.

"Really?" His mom said in wide eyes

"Your very beautiful girl, I bet Ashton have many rivals already!" His dad playfully and throw a smirk to his son.

" We're just friends!" Finally I voice out my thoughts

"Huh? Who?" Sofia asked.

"Ashton and me were just friends!" I said to clarify the information.

"Ouch I thought your going to be my daughter now" his mother said like she was in pain. I can see she wanted to cry.

"Mom, dad that's enough! We are getting to know each other for now" then hold my hand softly. But I glared at him since his parents are staring at us

"I never knew that a day will come that I can see my son being gentle and corny cheesy to a woman!" His dad snark a remark to his son.

"Dad.. please!" Ashton whine

"Dear do you like the appetizer?"

"Yes Sofia it's very delicious!" I answered

"Oh next time, come early and we can cook together. I never had any moment where me and a daughter to cook together since I only have a son. And he doesn't like to cook together with me too. So please fullfil my dream and cook with me!" She said in a hopeful smile.

"I will try Sofia!"

"Don't try let's do it. How about tomorrow?" She asked me in a gleeful sound.

"Umm I will try to since I don't know my schedule yet!" I said

"Oh...." I saw how her eyes shows disappointment. So I take back my words and said instead.

"I will come tomorrow" I said and I smile to her.

Ashton and his father smile to me.

"Thank you.... Thank you so much my daughter!" Then she ran into my arms and hug me..

Chapter twenty one

A shton POV

Having her in our house, eating dinner with my family is a blissful feeling. I once dream this will happen but now it's happening, I can't help but to feel overwhelmed. I just love this woman beside me. I can't wait to make my wife.

After eating dinner, we bid goodbye to my parents. She said she need to get home early. I reluctant to send her home since I really wanted to have her for myself.

When we are in the hospital parking area. She suddenly face me and look straight into my eyes.

"Ashton thank you for the dinner, I enjoy it" she said.

"Don't worry , mom ask you to cook together tomorrow right? I will come and pick you up" I said smiling excitedly

"Ashton about that... I think it's not appropriate to be close to your family. And I want to talk to you now" she said. " Can we sit in the bench on side?" She said. I obeyed her and take a sit beside her.

"Ashton about the past....." Before she could finished I cut her out and grab her hands tightly.

"I'm sorry... I know I am asshole, jerk, devil, bastard name whatever stupid name for me, that's I am in the past. But believe I regretted what I did to you. If I have a power to change what happened in the past, I will. Please for forgive me. I will do anything for you to forgive me" I said while hold her hand so tightly and look into deeply in her eyes, pleading for her forgiveness.

"I already forgive you, but we can't be the same anymore. I mean, don't visit me here or ask dinner together. I enjoyed the dinner with your family, thank you but that's it, I can't continue to meet you again!" She said while she try free her hands from my grasp.

"Please don't say that... Look I know I hurt you badly but please let me meet you. Don't forbid me to see you. Can't you see I like you more even I love you so much. Please give me a chance!" I said to her. Her words cut deeply in my heart. She said she doesn't want to see me.

"Ashton no! I think it's the best not to see each other. And I don't believe you love me maybe you just feel pity or sorry of what happened in the past. Just move on... I am ok and I am not hurting anymore" what the hell was that?

"What pity are you talking about? I am not... Look I have been searching for you for five years. The moment you walked out in that house that's the time I felt my heart chattered. I hurted you but it end up hurting me pretty badly. I lose you.... Everyday I always cry because of my stupidity. Please give me a chance... I promise this time I will not hurt you" I said while I kneel down without caring of anyone could see us.

"Get up Ashton, please don't make this hard for the both of us. I do love you in the past but right now I don't feel the same way anymore. I think it's the best to forget everything and move on!" She said while she grab me to help me stand but I stood in my place instead of standing I held her waist and embrace her while I rested my head on her lap.

"I love you so much please give me a chance. This time I will not be stupid, this time I will make things right. I will love and cherish you just what you deserve!" I can't help crying for her.

"Ashton no! I can't... Just forget everything. It will be the best!" Then she get up. No! No! I will not let her leave me again.

"Please babe!!! Have mercy on me. Please please.... Look" I hold her hand and put it in my chest. "Look can you feel? It's my heart.... It's beating so loud as if it explode when I am with you" I said while I plead for her.

"No...." She give me a serious face

"You can't do this... Please let me love you. It's ok if you don't love me. I will try my best to make you fall for me. I promise I will do anything. If you want I will be your slave... I will do it. Just give me a chance... One more chance and I promise you will not regret it. I will make you happy" I said while I try to console her more. I don't want to lose her.

"That's final... I can't. Find someone else Ashton!" She then turn away from me. But I run to her and hug her tightly. I even rested my head on her neck. I just want her so badly.

"Why can't you see? I love you... I love you so much... Please just a chance then you will not regret it. Babe please have mercy on me. If you want let's get married instead. How about that? Let's get married.... That's how serious I am to you!" I said while I still hold her while crying into her shoulder.

She wiggle as if she wanted to be out of my hold. She hold my face and make me look at her.

"I had loved you in the past... Those days when we are together you made me happy. But I hope you understand that I can't love you the same again. My heart has been broken by you and you have to understand I can't love you back again. I will not allow it to happen. It's my mistake that I fall for you. So please forget it... What you feel right now is not real. Go and look for someone that is right for you" she said then leaving me.

I frozed in my spot. She loved me before?? She did? Then it must had hurt and pain for her especially what I done to her. I let out a series of course. I look into the hospital she's working. Their is no way I will forget my feelings for her. Now that I know she had loved me then I will make her fall in love with me again.

This time I'll make sure that we will end up happily together forever.

chapter twenty two

Arabella POV

It's hurting me to say that words to him but I have to protect myself from him. He's not a good person to be with and I don't want to be played for a fool again.

I let out a big sigh and try to relax in my queen size big. It's my day off today and I am enjoying this day for myself.

I am planning to clean my apartment, go to grocery store and eat ice cream while staying in bed the whole time and tune in to Netflix.

Yes! I live separately with my parents. I want to be independent and thank God my parents especially my brothers agreed when I asked them that I want to live on my own. But even though they agreed, they keep visiting in my apartment every now and then talk about over protective again. But I just let them be, since I know they are right anyway.

I get up and push the blanket aside to step out in my bed. I hurriedly went to my washroom to do my business and take my shower.

I changed into my comfortable clothes since I will spending my time out of hospital. So casual will be fine for now. I let my hair down and wear my flip top.

I went outside and drove my car to the nearest McDonald's. I been craving for it lately, since I don't have much time to stop. Being doctor, you need to pour all your attention to your job. Can't afford mistakes since its life that we are saving.

After eating breakfast, I drove to the grocery store. The lines are pack and people are busy picking up their stuff. I went to ice cream section and choose my ever favorite flavor of all time, mocha chocolate with peanut and marshmallow, just exactly I love.

But before I could grab the ice cream container, a hand bet me to it. I look up and saw a girl, a pretty little girl.

"This is mine" she hissed at me.

"Ok, it's yours.. " I just need to grab another one though other flavor.

"Thank you!" She smile to me.

"Welcome little girl" I said while I smiled to her in respond.

"Hey Katie what are you doing in there?" A familiar make voice I heard at the back of the girl.

"Hey Ashy...!" Oh no... Not again..

He appeared on the back of the girl and when he noticed me, he look shock and then he regain his compose, then he smiled at me.

"Ara small world huh? What are you doing here?" He asked me while she look at me closely especially my basket where still empty.

"I bet her in getting ice cream Ashy... Hehehehe!" The little girl giggled to us

"Oh! You love ice cream too huh? By the way, this is my niece. She's my mom sister daughter Katherine, you can call her Katie for short. And Katie this is Arabella" Ashton introduced us to each other.

"Hi pretty girl" I said then I shake her little hands to mine.

"Your beautiful and very pretty. Are you Ashy girlfriend?" She asked me innocently

I shake my head in respond and look into Ashton whose looking to us.

"Nope! We are just friends" I said to her.

"Ouch... Ashy.. You should make her your girlfriend, she's very pretty and you both suit each other" she said to us while her eyes travelled to me to Ashton.

"Hahaha... Sorry about her, she's very talkative!" Ashton said while laughed awkwardly.

"It's true... Do you want to come with us? We're going to have little party in my house. Don't worry a lot sweet foods will be serve" she said as she invited me.

"Ops.. maybe next time... I still need to do things in my house" I said while I caress her cheeks affectionately.

"Really? But I like you though... Your so kind, not those other pretty girl they are so mean!" She said while she pout her cute lips.

"Ashton... I need to go. I need to grab few things for my house. See you next time little girl!" I said then I turn around walking away from them.

"Arabella... Take care" Ashton shout to me.

"You too both" I said then leaving then behind while I ready my basket.

After I am through with the things I need to put in my basket. I went to the cashier to pay the bills but the line is too long. I sigh and I line instead.

"Ara... You can line with us" Ashton said. I look at up to him whose on the other line but more close to the cashier. I shake my head since I don't want to be unfair for other customers who followed the rules in lining to pay in the cashier.

"Thanks... But I think I need to line Ashton!" I said while I stay put in my place.

"Come on!" Then he grab my basket in my hand. He put it in the counter since they are already in the cashier.

After the cashier finish, I was about to hand my card but Ashton bet me to it.

"I will pay for it!" Then he hand his card to the cashier.

"Ashton...!" I was about to protest.

"That's ok Beautiful, he have many many money...hehheh.." the little girl Katie said to me.

I waited for them to finished since I don't want to impolite. He paid for my groceries so I decided to wait for them. After awhile they finished and Ashton grabbed all the plastic paper.

"Ashton..." But before I could finished my sentence, he walked away heading towards the exit. Leaving me and Katie.

"Come!" I said to Katie while she hold my hand and we walked together.

When were almost in the parking area. I saw Ashton waiting in his car side.

"Thank you for paying and for carrying my belongings" I said to him as I grab the plastic bag.

"My mom called, I told her that Katie and I meet you here. She asked me to invite you. Please?" He said

"Pretty please... I really really like you. Can I play longer with you? Please? I promise to be good girl" she said while she make a promise sign on her cute little hand.

I shrugged and take a deep breath.

"Fine! I will come" I said while I smiled to Katie.

Ashton grab my bags again and guide us to his car. I am sitting in the passenger seat while Katie is on my lap. She said she doesn't want to go back seat.

Chapter tweenty-three

A shton POV

It's good thing Katie went with me in the grocery store cause she help me big time in convincing Arabella to come in my house.

"Your so pretty, are you a princess?" Katie asked her. My little keep staring at her and bouncing her lap.

"Nope of course!" She said laughing to Katie statement.

"She so pretty right?" I said fitting in their conversation.

"Eyes on the road Ashy" hahahah my little niece is kind of brat.

"True!" Arabella said as she giggled. She might find it funny that my niece scolded me.

"What do you do?" Katie asked her

"I'm a doctor" Arabella said as she beamed towards Katie

"Really? You have super power then?" My niece asked innocently

"Hahahah... Nope! It's my job to save people lives but I don't have any super power" she said smiling sweetly to my niece.

"Do you have a boyfriend?"

"Nope" she answered

"Then you can be Ashy girlfriend then, he doesn't have one. Mommy Sofie said Ashy is alone and sad that's why I went to his room and drag him to get me ice cream!" Wow she just said that to Arabella.

"What grade are you little girl?" Arabella said trying to avoid the topic, I see.

"Oh I am grade 2, I have many many friends" Katie said proudly.

"I bet, since you are a friendly beautiful girl" Arabella said to her.

"So will you be Ashy girlfriend please?" Arabella look at me but not answering the question. Katie look at her in hopeful eyes.

"Hmm.. Ashy and I are just friends Katie no more than that" she said. I glance at her sadly.

My car arrived in my parents house and I open the drive seat. I hover around my car to help Arabella with my niece.

While we're walking towards the house. I hold her hand while she glared at me

"I love you please give me a chance" I said to her.

"Shout up Ashton Katie will hear you"

"So?"

"It's embarrassing" she ask I can clearly see her cheeks turn pink.

"Your so beautiful, I can't wait to make you my wife" I said then she look at me annoyed and shake her head.

"Oh my God, Arabella your here dear?" My mom as she hug Arabella. I didn't my mom went near to us.

"Yes, Katie asked me to" she said softly

"Good thing! Because I miss you dear. How about we cook in the kitchen while the boys will prepare the table outside" my Mom while she look at me.

"What?" I asked her

"Go with your father and prepare the table in the garden" she said to me.

"Ok" I turn to Arabella and I sneak my hand to her small waist. " Love you babe" then I wink at her and walked away

Haizt, when will I get her? Can't she see I am so crazy about her.

I look for my dad and I saw him playing mobile legend on his phone. I shake my head, this guy have been childish ever since he retired from work.

"Dad your too old for that!" I scowl at him

"Whose old? I can give you a baby sister or brother at my age son" he said proudly.

"Really?" I asked sarcastic sound.

"Yeah, but its more better if you give us grandchildren instead" He said playfully while still playing his phone.

"I intend to do that dad, I just wait Arabella to say yes to me. She said she forgive me but she doesn't want to have relationship with me" I said while I plop myself in the sofa.

"Awwww... Never I emagine my son got a problem dealing with woman huh? I heard woman fluke at you like your a fish" my dad humor me.

"I don't care about those women. They are pain in the ass. I only have my eyes on Arabella" I answered him

"You must make her yours son, I bet a lot of boys already line up for her. Anyway Archer will never give her daughter to anyone else just easy. Arabella is a walking clone of her wife, hahahahah that guy is so madly in love with his wife" my dad laughed still his hand busy tapping on his phone.

"Then what shall I do?" I asked as I try to look my eyes in the ceiling.

"You had her once, definitely you can have her twice again. But this time, make it right. I think she just afraid. Persuade her more and broke her defense so she will open again to you" dad said. Wow! I look my dad amaze and smiling.

"Thanks dad! I never thought I could confine my problems and feelings to you this way. Thank dad" I said as I get up and hug him. Then I remembered, shit my mom will kill me if she find out we're not doing her command.

"Dad, mom asked us to prepare the table in the garden. I think she wants us to eat there" I said to him

"Why didn't you said earlier?" My dad said to me dumbfounded

"I will be grilled by your mom, let's go" he said then he put his phone aside. I shake my head as we exited the room. "Come on stop smiling like an idiot there" dad said loudly

"But dad I am not idiot!" I said to him

He just laughed at me as we went outside.

After we finished preparing the tables we sit down. I pour water in the two glasses and hand one to my dad.

"I'll be in the kitchen dad, I think I need some snacks" I said then I get up from my seat.

"Oh come, you just want to look at her" dad said while his eyebrows wiggle at me playfully

"You really know me" I said laughing and went to the direction of kitchen. I stop in my tracks, as I saw the beautiful sight I ever seen. my breath hitch that it almost stop for a second there.

Arabella wearing apron and simply doing her thing without noticing her sorrounding. Her forehead with a slight swear on it but boy her sight is so sexy.

Chapter twenty-four

Arabella POV

I am currently sitting in my dad study room waiting for my mom and dad to come down to their room. They called me early in the morning they said they want to discuss something very important to me. As a good daughter, I hurriedly went to my parents house thinking its important since my dad will never called me that kind of urgent.

While I am still waiting for them . I remembered the event happened yesterday. I thought taking a day off will cool off my mind from my work and Ashton but unluckily the boy appeared in front of my very eyes early in the morning and I was able to come with him to his parents house. So much for avoiding him.

Cooking and baking are my other passion aside from my work. I love the smell of fresh baked cake, cookies and brownies they are my most favorite sweet food in the world. Cooking also vegetarian food and yummy dishes keeps my tummy happy. Don't get me wrong for a woman like me whose never get fat even I eat the whole meat or sweet. Yes I don't get fat easily and thats makes me so lucky.

I feel my body shivered down to my spine as I continued mixing the ingredients in the pan. I know someone watching my every move since I can feel an eye bored in my back. I look up and try to catched the culprit. As I look up I saw Ashton leaning on the door with a creepy smile on his face. What's with him? I asked myself.

When he saw me looking at him, he smiled and walked towards me. He grab the stool and sat beside me. But he never uttered any single words while I am still busy mixing. I glanced to him and I caught him staring again.

"Ashton it's creepy when you look like that" I said to him. It's kind of awkward when someone look at you like your a food to eat.

"Why? You look so beautiful in that apron and I just having my imagination here" he said then a grin can be visible in his lips.

"Stop it" as I snapped at him and I raised my eyebrows to him.

"Come on! I just to have this moment. Like your my wife and I come home to see you looking like this" he said to me.

"Your weird I swear!" I said to him.

"Hey what are you both whispering there?" His mom said. I nearly forget that we are not alone, his mother is here with me cooking.

"I'm telling Arabella, how beautiful she is while cooking mom" he said. I glared at him since it's kind of embarrassing how easy for him to say that to his mom.

"Aww... Your my sweet boy! Arabella please have mercy on my son. I think he's crazy for you already" his mom said to me while she laughed softly and continued what she doing.

"See even my mom can see, how I am crazy for you" he said to me. "Why can't you not believed me when I said I am madly in love with you?" He continues

I just shrugged and continued what I'm doing. It's useless talking to him, I can't argue him about this matter.

"Babe I am going to make you love me again. Even if not you are going to be mine by hook or by crook since you are already mine anyways" he said then left me.

His words taunted me and I feel happy that I know he loves me. But I can't give up my defense and trust him again. I am afraid he might hurt me again. I don't want to be in that position again, just the thought of it make my heart in pain.

"Sweetie" my mom greeted me. I look into my mom whose looking as beautiful as ever. A lot of people said that I am exactly a carbon copy of her. But it's hard to believed, she's so beautiful and me? I look into myself and I saw only simple girl. My mom is so sophisticated and beautiful, even in her age, a lot of men still hinting her. That's why my dad never allowed her to be alone well except when she's in the hospital. Dad never trusted any guy, he will go berserk when he saw my mom talking to other guy.

"Mom" I stood up and kissed mom on her cheeks. " Your so beautiful mom" I said as I compliment her.

"Sweetie what are you talking about? You look like me, look at you" she said while she point myself.

"Hahahah.. mom that's impossible. I don't see any resemblance of you in me. I am slowly think that I am the ugly version of Ysabella Martin" I said dramatically.

"Princess don't ever said that. You are the most beautiful woman on earth. Hmm.. second to your mom. Of course!" Dad said playfully to us. While he hug me and kiss my mom on the lips.

"Dad what's this meeting all about? I went here early since you said it's very important" I said while we took a sit in the couch.

"It's about you" Dad said as he begin.

"Me? Why? Something wrong?" I said confused

"No their is no wrong, actually I asked your mom and your brothers about this. And they said it's a good idea since we will be assured that you will be in good hand" my dad said to me. As he try to look deeply to me.

"What do you mean?"

"We arrange you to marry Xavier. You know your Aunt Emma and Uncle Xavier son. They are so happy about it since it's you" Dad said to me. And my eyes almost pope out.

"Dad I can't marry Xavier... He's like my brother to me" I said to them

"Honey I know! But you come to love him eventually later. Me and your mom came from that. Look at us now, we are madly in love with each other" Dad explained to me like it's simple thing on earth.

"Dad.. I can't marry him. Please.. I am still young and please let me choose someone I love dad mom" I plead to them.

"Arabella.. we already broke this news to the public and right now I'm sure it's already out in the newspaper. You both still have plenty of time anyway. We give you three months to get married" my dad said to me.

I stand up and glared at him.

"You can't do this dad! I thought I am your princess? Why are you giving me away?" I said while my eyes started to form tears. I keep blinking to stop it from falling.

"Honey please cry! Archer... I already told you this is a bad idea. Look what you done?" My mom said angrily.

I swatted my mom hand as she try to hold me. I glared both of them as I grab my bag ready to leave this place.

"There's is no way I will get married dad mom. To hell with it" I said.

"Young lady don't ever raise that kind of tone to us. Xavier and me are business partner for so long. I want you to be in good hand and also it's good for the business too. The hospital also part of our partnership, just look at the big picture here. It's a win win situation for us both family" dad still trying to convinced me

"To hell with your business. I am resigning from the hospital. I will not marry Xavier dad even if you kill me. I won't!" I said as I stomp away from them. I cried as I went inside my car.

I drive to my apartment and lock myself in my room. I can't believed they do this to me. My phone keeps beeping it's a call from mom, dada and my brothers but I don't picked it up. To hell with them. They can't dictate my life.

Chapter twenty-five

Ashton POV

Monday morning I swear it's always been busy. My assistant entered my office with a cup of coffee in his hand. He put in my table as I busy signing some important papers.

"What's the schedule for today James?" I asked him

" General meeting in the conference room at 10 am sir

Lunch meeting with Mr. Backer

Opening ceremony in our newest branch this 4pm in the afternoon.

You have meeting with Mr. Guevara for the new location of the hotel sir at 2pm in the afternoon" James said.

"Ok thank you. Please kindly remind me of the time since I will be busy signing and reading this papers in my table. And don't forget to send flowers to Doc. Arabella in her office too" I said while I sip my coffee.

"Ok sir! I already done sending flowers to Miss Arabella sir!" He said

"You may take your leave then" I said as I dismiss him.

As he exited in my office his phone rang and he immediately went outside to answered it.

After a few moments, James came back with a newspaper in his hand and he seem to be a little agitated and nervous.

"What" snapped at him since I have no time to leasure around since I have a pack schedule today. I am planning to asked Arabella for dinner tonight so I need to finish all of this at once.

"Sir I believe they're a problem" he said while he keep gulping nervously.

"Problem? Spit it out James I don't have time for this!" I barked out loud.

"Sir the delivery said that Me Arabella is no longer working in the hospital" I look at him in confusion. Then he put the newspaper in my table. "Sir this, today's news said that arabel... I mean... Sorry sir... Ms. Arabella is engaged to be marry by Mr. Xavier Knight, her dad long time partner son in business" James said as I stuttered talking to me.

My eyes immediately snap and I read the news quickly. I tore it by pieces as I throw it in the floor.

For crying out loud, she can't marry that guy. She have me, I won't let that happen. Arrange marriage? What the fuck is that? Where not in the 21 century anymore.

I massage my head as I think of a way to solve this problem. There is no way I let Arabella marry that guy. Even if I have to kidnap her I will rather do that, than seeing her getting married to another guy other than me.

"James call my pilot and tell him that get my plane ready. I will need it today at anytime" I said as I stomp out from my office and dial Arabella number. But my phone went to her voicemail. I frown and I feel something is not right. She's not the type of person to marry someone she doesn't love. For sure this marriage is all about business. Fuck! Even if I have to give up my entire fortune and business I will just to stop that so called wedding.

I drive my car and head to her apartment. I caught up her mother at the door step of her apartment whose keep knocking on her door. She look at to me and I greeted her.

"Good morning Mrs Martin" I greeted her.

"Oh are you here for Arabella? Is she seeing you? Are you dating her?" Her mom bombard me with questions.

"Yes I came for her and I am courting her" I answered her all honesty.

"Oh God! If she open to you. Please tell her I love her. I will try to convince her father to cancel it. I leave her to you" she said then walk away.

"Bella? Babe? Open the door or I will break it!" I said as I try to knock many time but she never open.

"Babe please... Open the door, we need to talk? Come on lets talk babe!" I said to her.

"What?" she snapped angrily to me. thank god she opened her door. I hugged her tightly to my embraced. I kissed her forehead as I hold her both shoulder to face me. Her face is wet of tears and her eyes are red and swollen, she must have crying for long time. I felt tug pain in my chest I saw her state. I hug her again and I patted her back softly as I calm her down.

"Don't ever make me worry like that ever again woman. I almost died for worrying you" I said to her. Then I caress her cheeks and wipes the tears that rolls in there.

I guide her to the sofa and make her sit beside me.

"Why? What happened?" I asked her as she settled in her seat.

"They want me to marry Xavier" she said to me. While she cry again.

"Why?" I asked her although my heart wanted to explode.

"They said it's about business since Dad and uncle Xavier has been business partner and they said it will be better just to merge everything, since we are going to be real family when I get marry to Xavier" she said while she cry as she spoke.

"Babe, I will asked you one question. You answer me honestly ok?" I asked her and I stared at her carefully. She nodded to me. And I inhale and exhale.

"Do you want to get married to him?" I asked her looking at her without blinking at eyes.

"No" she said immediately

"Do you love him?"

"No!" She said and I smiled to her responsed. Thank God!

"Which one do you prefer me or him?" I asked her. She look at to me shock.

"I don't Ashton... All I want is to fullfil my dreams. I don't want to get marry yet. We are both young too. I don't want to rush decision in marrying it's a lifetime commitment" she said to me.

"Then what is your dream?"

"I want to be a doctor... A good doctor like my mom" she said.

"I will stop you for doing what you love babe! Heck I will even support your dreams. Let's get married please... I don't want any other guy claiming you" I said to her.

"But....." I stopped her and kissed her senselessly.

"I love you so much... Do you love me?" I asked her as I rest my forehead to her. She nodded to me and she blushed. I smiled and kiss her again.

"Say it please...!!" I plead.

"Yes I also love you!" She said her cheeks is crimson red at the moment.

I kissed her passionately then the kiss turn to hungry one. I snake my hands underneath her shirt and caress her stomach up to her breast. She gasped making her lips parted a little I plunged my tongue inside her as I tasted every corner of her mouth.

We continued till the very last drop of our clothes. I kissed her neck down to the valley of her breast. I pull up and stared at her body. Fuck! She's fucking sexy and she's mine. She blocked her hands to her nakedness and quickly get up but I did not allow her.

"Ashton I think it's wrong...!" What wrong is she talking about?

I push her again in the bed and I hover her without responding to her. I trap her by putting my hands on each side of her head.

"This is right... Your mine babe!" I said then I captured her sweet lips again. My hands travel to her breast as I massage it gently.

(Can't continue sorry... Just imagine the rest..heheheheh...)

After we made love many times I drew her in my eyes since she already passed out. Hahahahah my poor baby I made her exhausted and tired. I kissed her forehead lovingly and I closed my eyes, enjoying the blissful moment together and I fall to my deep slumber.

chapter twenty six

Arabella POV

I lay down in my bed as I recall what happened yesterday. My God I was having sex with Ashton in my apartment. Just the thought of it makes me blushed. What did I think that I did that? What's gets inside my head at that time? Am I paranoid or something?

I passed out after several times of love making with him. Shit! Did he wear protection? My God why I did not think of it. Shit!

I beep sound halted me from my stupid thought. I lift my phone and I saw a message came from Ashton.

"Babe, I will have few things to do. Do not go outside or do something ok? I know you are sore and tired of what happened. I'll be back after I done! Would like me stop by from a shop to get you something? What do you want to eat?" He asked me.

I ignored it and sigh deeply. I decided to get up and wash my body since I can smell scent of Ashton in me.

I walked to the washroom and I strip my clothes one by one. As I glance in the mirror, I frown when I noticed something in my body, especially in my neck? What's that? I stared at it and eyes went wide as big as the flying saucer.

"What the heck? A hickeys!!! My god I can't even count how many they are. My god that idiot is impossible" I exclaimed while I look into the mirror.

I shake my head and let it be, there is no used complaining anyway since it's already been done. I just need to cover this hickeys when I decide to come out in my house. I proceed to take my bath and feel the warmness of the water in my body.

As I exited the washroom door, I heard my phone ring and answered it.

"Sweetie thank God, you pick up.. please come here in your dad's office now!" My mom said panicked

"Mom if it's about the marriage, I can't! Please talk to dad about it ....." Then I heard a chattered and broken sound and I can even heard a loud voice shouting. I think it's my dad.

"Mom what happened in there? Why did I heard som...!" My mom cut me off and said.

"Come here this instant, Ashton have been beaten by your dad and your brothers" my mom said while she shouted stop to stop them.

I didn't bother to say goodbye to my mom and I hung the phone immediately. What did that idiot do in my dad office? Most especially with my brothers?

My mind have been running wild as I panicky changed into my clothes. I run to my car and drove as fast as I can in my dad office or rather shall I say in our house.

As I entered the house, I heard shouting and shattered broken or bang sound again. I felt chest tight and I am getting nervous as I am getting closer to the my dad's office.

"Dad no!" I shout as I run to rescue Ashton who is now half beaten by my family. I look at him and I saw a lot of cuts and bruises to his body.

"What have you done dad?" I asked my dad angrily

"How dare you defend that brute. Do you think I didn't knew about what he done to you back then? Remember when you cried and asked us to transfer you to other place? Other school? I am not stupid" my dad said angrily as he punch his table.

"We knew everything Arabella do not ever defend that guy to us!" Daniel said to me.

"I am not defending him or deny it. But you can't do this to him for goodness sick! How you beaten him? The three of you? How could you?" I said angrily while I am crying in front of them.

"Babe don't cry, I am ok please it's my fault and I deserve it. I should have gotten this before" Ashton said as he try to get up. But he whimper as he try to move.

"Shout up!! Why did you ever go here in the first place?" I scolded him.

"I just want to make things right and clear to them!" He said

I help him get up and put him in the couch. My mom hand me a first aid kit and I automatically treated Ashton bruises and cuts.

"Get him out of the house now!" My dad hissed.

"Archer I swear I am going to leave the house of you do that!!! How could you say such a thing like that? Look at your daughter she's the one whose hurting here!" My mom said. My dad softened a little when my mom said "leave"word.

"Honey, that guy played and toyed her, how can she trust him again?"

"Get up" as Daniel said while he about to lounge to Ashton.

"No" I said then I put myself in the middle of them. "Touch him again and I will hate you Daniel" I said angrily

"Don't you dare!" Emman said to me and he went closer too.

"What did you see to this guy huh? How could you forgive him just like that?" Daniel hissed to me.

"Do you know why we want you to get marry Xavier? Because of him" as he point to Ashton. " We knew he keep bothering you again so in order for him to be out of the picture we decided to marry to Xavier!" Emman said to me.

I aware I never been feel very angry as what I felt right now. How could they do this to me.

"You don't have the right to do that to me. You may my brothers but I am still older than you. How could you treated me that way! You marry me off? For what? To be away from him? Why can't you mind your own business? This is my life, I am grown enough... What happened in the will remain in the past. It's my choice to choose him not you, nor not to dad or mom. I will choose who I will marry whether you like it or not!" I said to them shouting.

"Oh God! Honey calm down" my mom said as she ran closer to me and embraced me. "Shhhhhhh..... It's ok.. it's ok...you don't have to cry" as she calm me down. She snap around and look into them.

"Be a man the three of you. If you want to fight, fight him one by one not this way. How could beaten him the three of you? I raised you to be better both Daniel and Emman but I am very disappointed!" My mom continue "and you , you sleep in the guest room I don't want to see you near me! I had enough of your stupidity!" My mom burst crying.

I saw how my dad change face into calmer one. Even my brothers did the same. They all can't stand my mom crying. We all do.

Chapter twenty seven

Ashton POV

I expected this to happened to me when I voluntarily went to Arabella's parents house being beaten by her brothers and dad. But I didn't regret anything at all. I want to fight for her. I just can't stand the fact she will get married to other guy.

The reason why I went there because I want to talked or negotiate to them. Arabella said that one reason why his father want her to marry Xavier because of the business. So I proposed to them.

I took a sit as I ready myself. I knew they don't like me I can see the way they stared at me.

"What are you doing here?" Archer said, Arabella father.

"I am here sir because I want to bargain a merger of our company to yours" I said calmly

"What makes you think we want to merge with your company?" He said while I can sense a light raised in his voiced

"Sir, I am proudly say that our business is good just like yours. We also have same market value so I think it's a good between both parties"

"No!" He said.

"Then sir, please let me buy the entire hospital business of yours" I said calmly

"What? Are you out of your mind? What are you? Are you crazy?"

"Sir, Arabella resign because she doesn't want to work under your company, so I want to buy the hospital business and I want to name it to her" I said.

"What gives you the right to say that huh?" Daniel said to me while he bang the table in front of me.

"Because I love her and I want to make her happy. If she doesn't want to work there because of what happened then I will buy it so she can work again. She's happy being a doctor and I want her to continue to be that way!" I was about to wiped the sweats in my forehead, a suddenly a hand punch me right in my face. Then lounge at me , the three of them and the rest is history.

Right now, I am in Arabella's bedroom in there house after she dragged me here. (Not that I complaining). She's busy treating my wounds but me being the idiots who keeps staring at her especially in her exposed cleavage. (What horny little fella I am). But can't blame me ok? She's very very sexy in her outfit. I swear this girl will make me horny effortlessly. I swear she doesn't have any slight idea how my mind works right now especially when she flip her hair to the other side. My God I want to bite that neck again. I smiled proudly as I saw my mark on her. (Heckys looks good on her)

"Ashton can you please stop smiling? It's creepy you know! You are being beaten the shit of you and you are now here smiling like idiot. Are you crazy?" She hissed at me.

"I am just happy babe..."

She look at me dumbfounded

"Happy because you got beaten?" She asked wildly

" Hahahah.. babe of course not! But if being beaten that I will able to see looking like that and worried about me. I will be gladly volunteer to be beaten babe!" I said while I try to stretch my arms to hug her but before I could do that a hand swatted me.

"Get off your hands to my sister you fucker!" Daniel said while he sit down in the couch near the bed.

"Daniel please no fighting!" Arabella warn him

" I am not here to fight I am here to guard you. Just look at your boyfriend he's been smiling and grinning while he looks at you. Can't you see he's thinking the other way?" Her brother said.

"Ashton!!!" She glared at me.

"Babe??? What?? I didn't do anything!!" I said then went to embraced her.

"I said it off idiot!" Emman said this time

My God this guys are so annoying. Don't tell me they are going to block me from their sister?

"Haizt guys can you leave? This is my room!" She said like she's stating an obvious.

"Yup we knew but you do realize you have your boyfriend inside together with you? We don't want him to attack you while we are there outside!" Daniel said.

"Come on don't tell me your going to be cock blocker even when we are married!" I asked them dramatically as I put my hands on their sister shoulder.

"Cock blocker?? Huh? Married? Who says we allow you?" Emman said to me.

"Guys please, stop it ok? Your both over reacting again" she said as she put the kit in the drawer. Then she look at the three of us.

"Over reacting? Look at your neck.. it's say how over reacting we are!" Emman hissed as he point Arabella neck. She then quickly hide her hickeys

"Useless to hide we already saw it. What happen after then? What if you get pregnant" Daniel said to her.

"So I can take care of the baby on my own ok? I am a doctor!" She said to them.

"Own? Baby? pregnant?Who says your going to it alone? Your not going to marry me?? As if I will let you!" I bursted out. Just the thought of it makes me angry.

"What pregnant? Whose baby?" Archer said. We didn't noticed her approached to us since we are busy arguing

"Oh my God sweetie! Your pregnant? Am I going to be a grandma soon?" Her mom said happily as she excitedly clap her hands.

"Can you all stop mentioning about the baby who doesn't exist? Please guys respect my choice" she told them while she sit beside me and I hugged without caring if her siblings will get angry.

"Why can't you not fall for Xavier? Not this guy?" Daniel said as he pointed me.

"What's wrong with me? I love your sister more than my life you know!" I said to them.

"Enough guys, give them a break! Come on let's seriously now" her mom said as she raised her eyebrows to her husband whose looking grumpy all the sudden.

"Fine! I will allow you to date my daughter Carter! But no more than, marriage is out of line" Her dad said. I should be happy that he already approved me but he said no marriage? The fuck?

"Thank you sir but with due respect my relationship with your daughter have an intention to get married. They're is no way, I will let your daughter go!" I said to them.

They all looked at me as if they wanted to read my mind. Then I noticed her mother smiled to them.

"Guys stop it ok? It's not that we are going to get marry now. Anyway we are just trying this relationship first" Arabella said to them and I look at her shocked.

"Ok that's Arabella to decide, I will leave it to her. But if you hurt her we will kill you Carter!" Her dad said finally.

"So???" She then asked them and eye them one by one as if they're communicating.

"Let's go down sweetie, let's prepare dinner" her mom said all the sudden. She look at me sternly

"Ok!!" She turn to me " Ashton I will go with mom, ok!" Then she look at the three of them " Daniel, Emman and dad please behave don't ever trash my bedroom like you do to your office" she then storm out together with her mom.

chapter twenty eight

Arabella POV

I am thankful that my family already softened and they accepted Ashton as my boyfriend. But even so, I am currently cooking with my mom for our dinner but my mind run with different scenarios of what's happening up there. I am too worried for Ashton.

"Hey come on, we didn't heard any broke glasses or shouting. They must have talk seriously. I will kill the three of them if they do" My mom said. I smiled to her. I am so thankful that I have my mom, she said she's happy for me but I should be careful since what happened in the past

"Thanks mom" I said then I proceed to my cooking.

After a long waiting the boys finally ascended down and I look at them. Ashton was being dragged by my brothers.

"Your heavy, what does my sister see in you!" Emman complain as he put him in the stool.

"I'm handsome right babe?" He answered then wink at me. I smiled then my smile died soon as I saw my two brothers playfully smack his head.

"What the?? Why are you both being violent? Can't I not wink on my girlfriend?" He look at them angrily as he swatted my brothers hands.

"I can't seem to digest this! My sister having a boyfriend whose the greatest idiot in the world" emman rolled his eyes and plop in the stool beside Ashton.

"Yeah idiot and a fucker! Why can't you not choose Xavier? He's handsome too!" Daniel complain again. But I just shrugged without bothering to answer them.

"Xavier? How about you marry his sister? What's her name again? Emmie? Dude you look good together!" Ashton said to him

"Leave Emmie out of this!" Then he smack Ashton again. I swear this guys is so violent with my boyfriend.

"What's with Emmie honey?" My mom asked Daniel teasing tone.

"Mom! It's nothing we just both hate each other. You know that right?" Daniel said while he snorted and type something on his phone.

"There is a thick line between hate and love Daniel.. for sure!" Ashton said laughing. I think this guy wanted to be dead tonight

"What did you say?" Daniel about to lounge him

"I am just joking ok? But anyway she signed contract in our company. At first I am shocked but she become ambassador to our hotel" Ashton said "I think she's going to have pictorial today... I bet I need to have a copy of the pictures I might send it to someone" he said playfully making my mom burst laughing.

"Shout up you idiot" Daniel said.

"I am so happy at least we have another addition to the family but sad at the same time since it makes four idiot in total to this house" my mom said laughing as I laughed to her joke too.

"Honey I am not idiot?" Dad said and hugged my mom as she still cooking in the oven.

"Whose in the right mind to trash his office? Only idiot can do that!!" My mom answered him.

"I swear, Arabella and your mom looks exactly the same even they are laughing" Ashton said in a amazed.

"We won't argue with you with that fucker" Daniel said

"Yeah I can agree with that!" Emman said as he look at us.

"Wow! For the first time you agreed to me??" Ashton said shocked

"Of course! They are both beautiful isn't it? " Emman said

"Dude you both are creep I think you both have brother complex" Ashton said wildly

"What did you say?" Daniel said to him glaring.

"I am just telling the truth ok? Your really attached to her. You know right, someday will going to get married whether you like it or not" swear this guy really have a death wish.

"Nah! She will not marry you!" Emman said calmly. I raised my eyebrows shocked. Wow! Thank God they are calm down now.

"What makes you think she will not marry me?" Ashton said to him. I think he's pissed off.

"Because she will come to realize that picking you is a mistake, your stupid and idiot" Emman said to him.

"I am not!!"

"Guys you all knew I am here ok? Can you drop that topic and help us arrange the table? So we can eat dinner now!" I said to them.

They all get up but Ashton winced in pain as he try to move. I walked to him and stop him.

"You can sit down there! That's ok leave the work to them" I said smiling

"Thanks babe!" Then he hugged me.

"Fuck off dude!" Emman said as he swatted Ashton arms on my body.

"My god! Can you please just do what you asked to do? Can't I hug my girlfriend?" Ashton said

"You do realize that before she became your girlfriend, she's out little sister?" Daniel said to him.

"Shit your brothers are all annoying" Ashton hissed complaining

"Come" then I offer my arms for him to support he then automatically put his arms around me " god you smell so nice" he said as he smell me.

"Weirdo I am smell mix of blood, sweat and food and you said I smelled nice? You must have problem in your sense organ Ashton" I said to him then I put him in the chair and I sit beside him.

We eat silently and then Ashton broke the silence for a moment.

"Sir, can I buy the hospital?" He blurted it out all the sudden.

"It's for her on the first place no need to buy. Maybe only the half since Xavier own the half of it. Emma doesn't have time to handle the hospital I will asked Xavier if he allowed to sell his part" my dad said.

"Why are you buying the hospital" I asked him

"Because I want to give it to you! You said you want to be doctor right? And you quit after what happened. So I will buy it so you don't have to quit" he explained to me while he resume to eat his food. I look at him shocked.

"Anyways, if you want to merge your company to ours it's up to you. Why did you asked anyway?" My dad said in curiosity

"You want Arabella to marry Xavier because he's the son of your Busan partner right? So I wanted to be your business partner too, so you will let me marry her" Ashton said like it's simple.

"Whipped idiot" Daniel mumbled as he continued to eat.

"Did your father agreed to this?" My dad asked him

"It's been three years I handle the family business and I proud to say that I expand it bigger and better from he expected. Also I am the only heir, so he said it's up to me. He doesn't argue anything at all since he's busy having vacation around the world with my mom" he said

"Tell your dad we can talked about it" dad said.

"So can I marry her sir?" Ashton said again

"Fuck you!" Emman said

"Idiot!" Daniel said in unison.

"No cursing when eating guy's" my mom reprimanded them.

"As I said it's up to her" my dad said pointing at me. And I smiled to him.

"You will marry me right? Babe?" Ashton said to me and he give me a puppy eyes.

"Idiot" my brothers said in unison again.

"Shout up, you just jealous because you don't have love life" Ashton said to them.

"Mom I think we both have headache since they're is another addition of the family whose childish and idiot as my brothers" I said laughing

"Babe I am not idiot. Your brothers are just too much" he said to me.

"Fine just eat your food, so we can go home"

"Home?" My brothers said in unison again

"Are you both living together in one house?" My dad asked me

"Of course not dad!" I said to them out loud.

" I swear Arabella if you living together with this guy I will shop his balls and feed it to the dogs" Daniel said

"Hey leave my balls alone, you want to be uncle right?" My god this guy have no shame at all.

"Ashton stop it it's embarrassing" I punch his side as I glared at him.

"But babe he started it again" he said to me.

Happy though my family finally accepted him but I am sad because another idiot will be add to our family.

Chapter tweenty-nine

Ashton POV

No words can express how happy I am. At last her family is not against us and right now I am in dilemma cause I been searching for a engagement ring that best suited to my love of life, my Arabella.

Though I am bit worried since this morning she keep throwing and she said she felt dizzy sometimes. I told her to go to the doctor and she just laughed at me.

"Haha.. Ashton you are really an idiot! Why would I look for a doctor when I am a doctor" she exclaimed to me while laughing.

"Yeah right , you are a doctor but your human too. You get sick, so you need to go to check up. I don't want to see get sick babe" I said to her as I rubbed her back trying to calm her since she keep throwing in the toilet bowl. I wipe her face and clean it using my handkerchief.

"You will be dead if my brothers saw you here in my apartment Ashton. Go home you practically living here" she said to me.

"But I like it when I am close to you. Eating and cuddling together is the best" I said while I smile to her lovingly

"You called it cuddling? When you don't even make me sleep or wink every night?" She said.

"Hahaha.. babe I can't help it . My girlfriend is so sexy. I can't seem to get enough " I said.

"But having sex in six times in a night? Is it normal?" She asked me

"Of course! We can even go beyond that!" Then I wink at her. She look at me in horror.

"Ashton no more than that! I swear I am gonna cut your balls" she said then she walked to the bedroom and lay down. While her hands in her forehead.

"You ok?" I look down on her.

"Yup! Maybe I just tired!" She ssid. While her eyes are closed.

"Babe let's go to the hospital" I said as I try to get her up.

"Don't worry ok? I will go to hospital and check up for now I will rest here and you go to your office" she said while she turn around and scoop the duvet to cover her body

"You sure babe? You want me to join you in bed?" I said as I whispered in her ears Making her blushed.

"Ashton.. I will call my brothers I swear and they will drag you out in my apartment" she threatened.

"Ok ok! No need for that! You know those brothers of yours they're too protective. Even I am your boyfriend" I complain while I changed into my suits. I saw Arabella staring at me.

"Babe,?..." I said to her

"Hmm?" She said then she blushed since I caught her staring at me. Cute!

I bend down and hover over her and kissed her passionately. Good thing she's still in her nighties I can easily get rid of it.

After a couple of love making. Arabella gets tired and exhausted making her fall asleep. I exited her apartment and went to my office.

"Sir how about this?" A flirty sales lady asked me. Waking me up from my thoughts

"Nope! She doesn't like that. My fiance is simple and kind" hmm. After looking around my eyes suddenly flicker as I saw a beautiful yet simple ring just want I wanted.

"That's one of the most expensive ring in our collection sir. It's limited edition" She said to me. I didn't miss how she try to brushed her boobs in my arms. I step backwards since I don't want to be called pervert or being attracted to her.

My God why can't this woman get it? Hitting on me is useless.

I love my girlfriend too much. And I can't cheat her she's the love of my life. My air that I breathe, my food and my salvation.

My phone ring and I frown my soon to be brother called me it's Daniel.

"Fucker! Where are you? Your girlfriend fainted" he said

"What? Why?where is she is she ok? My God, my God!" I said as I panicked.

"Calm down idiot, she's not waking up yet and we still waiting for the doctor. Go here now" then he hung up.

After I paid the ring I went to my car and speed driving till I reached the hospital. My chest keeps beating so loud .

As I approach her room, I saw her laughing together with her brothers.

"Hey are you ok?" As I come near her bed and I hugged the kiss her on lips . But a hand smacked me on my head

"Stop kissing my sister in front of us" " I rolled my eyes. Again this brother complex.

Arabella just laughed at us.

Then a doctor open the door with a paper on her hand.

"So the patient is ok.. don't worry! Hmm she got fainted because she has low blood and she's two weeks pregnant! Congratulations " she said smiling.

I hugged Arabella and kissed her. She smile to me. Then the doctor said we need to set appointment for gynecologist to examine both the mother and the child. Then she exited the room. Due to the happiness I felt I didn't noticed the dark aura on her brothers.

"You got my sister pregnant? Even you are not yet married?" Daniel shouted.

"You stupid idiot" Emman said as he about to lounge on me

"My God what happened here???" A door opened and reveals her parents.

"Arabella get fainted and she's pregnant!" Daniel said.

" You got my daughter pregnant Carter. I am going to kill you" her father said loudly booming every corner of the room.

"Say your prayers now idiot" Daniel said as he gets ready his fist for me.

" Stop it you three! You do realize that your sister and daughter is pregnant and you want to slaughter her boyfriend in front of her? Do you want your sister to get stress? Huh?" Her mom said.. thank God

"Of course not!" They all said

"Then good!! Congratulations baby" her mother said then she cried.

"Mom" all of them said unison.

"Honey!" Her husband said

"Sort I am just emotional my own baby having her own baby too. Archer we are getting old" she said as she wipes her tears

"Shhh... It's ok honey! Arabella will always our baby. Right sweetie??" Her dad said smiling though I can see faint tears on his cheeks.

Haizt this family they really love my girlfriend and soon to be wife and mother of my child.

"I am not a baby dad!" Arabella whined to them. "Stop treating me like one"

"Carterrrrrrr...." Her dad said out loud again. I flinched as I approach Arabella with a smile on my face. Thank God I already purchased a ring or else I will get grilled by her family.

"Babe! I am so happy to be a father and sorry I didn't able to prepare any long saying but I love you so much. I plan to propose to you in a romantic way but I guess I need to do this now or I will get grilled by your family!" I said then she laughed at me.

I took out the box in my pocket and opened it.

"Will you marry me?" I said as I kneel down in front of her. God I know it is embarrassing to propose right in front of your in-laws with a very awkward position too. But I need to do this since I love this woman so much.

She looked at me and she cried

"Yes I will marry you!" She said then I hugged her and kissed her.

Then we are being separated my a hand. They practically drag me and they hugged Arabella.

"Be careful baby sis!" Daniel said his tears almost drop.

"Tell us when that fucker hurt you ok?, We will kill him for you!" My God what a violent in law I have. I shake my head and just shrugged.

"Ashton don't ever hurt my baby girl. She's our one and only daughter. Make her happy. She's our little bundle of joy!" Her mom said crying.

"Hurt my baby girl or I will kill you Carter" her dad threatened me and patted my back. "Congratulations son! Welcome to the family" he said then all of her brothers hugged me and patted my back too. .

Gezz talking about bipolar much.

Whatever as long Arabella is going to be my wife. I am happy with it.

****

Next will be the last chapter and epilogue hope you guys love the story of Arabella and Ashton...

Chapter thirty

I want to dedicate this chapter to the three of you who always tune in for my latest updates.

user82274484

xoxo7a

Epilogue

Arabella POV

It's been ten years that Ashton and I got married. I still remembered how happy and blissful that day.

Ashton relay on me of all the preparation from gowns, foods, venue, cater service, church etc. He said.

"I want you to remember the day you said yes to me. So, all the decisions will only rely on you. Pick anything you love and I will do the rest. I want you to have your dream wedding"

That silly husband of mine. It's really tiring anyway since I only had to decide the rest of the planning goes to my mom and her mom. Both of our parents are happy that we end up together especially our mothers.

I choose my own gown which I really loved. It's very beautiful and simple. Ashton doesn't like revealing gowns because he doesn't want other men ogling me.

But even if he does allow me to wear revealing gown, I still don't like it. I still can recalled Ashton reaction when he saw me wearing very revealing gown in our fitting session for our wedding gowns.

After I try to fit it, I went outside to let Ashton see whether he like it or not. When he saw me his eyes almost out and his mouth drop.

"Don't you dare wear it Arabella. I swear were not going to church if you choose that dress " He said to me.

I laughed at him and he try to glared at me. I hugged him while I giggled

"You don't have to throw a fit. It's our mom pick you know, it's not mine. Heheh.." I said then he suddenly pull me to his body and I can smell manly perfume in my nostril. He bend down his head and kiss my ears down to my exposed shoulder. My eyes went wide when I realized we are not alone in the room. I saw our mom giggles looking on us.

"Ashton your lucky her brothers didn't show up or else they will drag you outside" my mom said while laughing.

He shakes his head and wink at me as exited to changed the gown.

Ashton father said to my dad that whatever Ashton decision about the company, it's up to him. He said he's the only son of mine and I think whether we merge or not our grand children will benefits of it.

Speaking of grandchildren after ten years we able to produced four children. Why? Blame my husband is so horny and always full of energy especially at night.

I had twins both girls in my first pregnancy. Both family are happy because my family wants another girl addition and Ashton family only have him so having two girls is the family ultimate wishes. I named them Ashley whose older than five seconds to Anna. They are both have my genes which makes my husband happy. I don't why but he prefer that my children will all look like me.

Ashley is Daniel little spoiled girl. When she's about one year old she always went to Daniel office. Hahahah.. she prefers her uncle company than her dad.

Anna on the other hand is Emman side kick. My brother loved that child like his own. He even bought her own customize Ferrari car for five years old just because Anna begging him to buy it for her. Talking about whipped uncle. Hahahah..

My twin girls are now 9 years old. They all both went to same school. And boys are having crushed on them but as usual my brothers are so strict, they are the one who pick them and drive them to school.

After my twin girls, I had again another twin boys. That makes me have four children total in all. I told Ashton that this will be my last pregnancy because I can't take it anymore giving birth to a two consecutive twins. Giving birth to them is suck and it hurts like hell.

My boys on the other hand are grandpa's boy. Hahaha yes! You heard me right. They love being with their grandpa. I name them Usher and Jasper.

My dad and Ashton dad are now best buddy they are buddies in playing sports that's why my twins love to be with them cause they said they're grandpa's are cool.

The two grandpa's are whipped by my boys. When my boys asked them to buy each pony. They literally bought ten horses so that the kids can pick anyone they like. They even bought a farm to put the horses there. The twins also made them bought tank fish, goats, chickens, turtles and ducks. I don't why but my two boys are fan of animals.

Both our mothers are sad since they can't spoiled they're grandchildren because of those idiots. They even beg for me to have a other pregnancy so they can have one too. Haizt!

Right now, I am cooking for dinner and waiting for my girls and boys to be arrived from school and of course for my loving husband too. All throughout the years he became very loving and sweet. He never failed to give me surprises even though we are too old for it.

"Mommy were home" The voice of my nine year old daughter Ashley.

"Mommy.....!!!" Anna said to me as she open her arms to hugged me.

My girls are loving and sweet just like their father.

"Anna, your not a baby anymore. Don't make mama carry you, your heavy" my son Usher said. Then he kissed me on my cheeks.

"Aww are you all home my children?" I said to them.

"Yes mommy!!! They all said

"Mommy I'm hungry what's for dinner?" Jasper asked me as he drop his bag on the couch and walk towards me then hugged me.

"Eww.. boys should not kiss mama" Ashley said to him.

"Who said?" Jasper and Usher said.

"Hey what's the commotion about my children's and my favorite sweet beautiful and sexy wife?" Ashton said to me as he bend down and kiss me on my lips.

"Dadddddddyyyy no kissing!" Ashley said

"Grossed!" As my boys snorted.

Then we eat out family dinner as we talked about things especially about their school.

"I have good news for all of you and guess what?" My husband said as he put his arms around me and kiss the side of my cheeks.

"Your going to buy us limited edition of Audi car?" Anna said. This girl and her obsession of cars.

"Your gonna buy me limited edition of Valentino bag that is newly lunch dad!" Ashley said. Haizt she and her girly stuff. She even have more bags than me. Blame it to Daniel.

"Nope! Ashley but I saw your Uncle Daniel purchased Valentino limited edition bag in our mall when I checked the branch today!" My husband said. Then Ashley all went to jumping and grab her phone . Yeah you guess it right she will call her beloved Uncle. Hahahah..

"You girls are all boring! Dad do you purchased a new lot and decided to make it a zoo?" Usher said as Jasper look at him too.. looks like he approved his brother suggestion.

"Son! You already have five hectares farm which field with different animals. Why do you want another one?" My husband asked them.

"Because animals are cool!" They both said together.

My girls cringe their nose in disgust.

"Ewww!" They both said.

"Boys and girls listen to your dad!" I told them as they about to argue again.

"We are all going to Greece, were going to family vacation" My husband said enthusiastically

"Then can grandpa's and grandma's can come too?" Jasper asked.

"Yes we will asked them, if they will like to come!" Ashton answered them

"We will call them father" my boys said as they jump and head to their bag to get their phone to call their grandparents.

"How about our uncle's?" Oh boy! My girls really are uncle's girl.

"If they have time since they are busy with the business" my husband answered.

"Daddy uncle Daniel said he will come!" Ashley said as she still talking to her uncle.

Oh boy this vacation will surely be fun!

I grin as I watched my husband.

"What?" I asked him

"Those fuckers will come and I bet they will cock block me again!" He said to me.

"Shhhh... Children will heard you!" I warn him.

"I have also surprise for you all!"I said to them.

Their eyes snap to me and anticipate my surprise.

" I am pregnant! We're going to have another addition to the family!"

I saw my children eyes grew wide.

"Oh my God mom! I hope they are all girls not boys!" Ashley said.

"Girls are sucks and picky. They are should be boys" usher said.

"They?" I asked them

"Your going to have another twin right mom?" My children asked me

I shake my head.

"No!"

"Babe I swear you are so cute" Ashton said to me.

"Ashton this will be the last. I swear I am going to cut your balls" I said to him

" But babe you love me right?"

I sigh as I look at them. My mother-in-law and my mother will be happy since this is what they wanted.

"That's ok babe! I grow into small family and it's very lonely. Having much children is fun. I love you babe thank you for giving me a bunch of happiness" aww.. this husband of mine.

"Ashton Carter you really knew how to softened my heart!" I said to him.

"Can't blame you I am irresistible" then he kissed me again.

"Daddddddyyyy!" All of my children said as we laughed together when pull out.

THE END

www.ingramcontent.com/pod-product-compliance
Lightning Source LLC
Chambersburg PA
CBHW072208070526
44585CB00015B/1247